My Schoolhouse Is A Ghost Town

A Teacher's Story Through Reform

SUNNI ALI

authorHOUSE®

AuthorHouse™
1663 Liberty Drive
Bloomington, IN 47403
www.authorhouse.com
Phone: 1 (800) 839-8640

Published by AuthorHouse 06/15/2016

ISBN: 978-1-5049-8509-3 (sc)
ISBN: 978-1-5049-8508-6 (hc)
ISBN: 978-1-5049-8507-9 (e)

Library of Congress Control Number: 2016904008

Print information available on the last page.

CONTENTS

ACKNOWLEDGMENTS

When falling into an unconscious slumber at night, I have great conversations with my kinfolk: Eva Mae Howard, William Fletcher Howard, my former teachers, Malcolm X, Dr. King, Booker T. Washington, Sojourner Truth— the list goes on. Of course, my favorite conversations are with my parents telling me I should write my thoughts down in a book to share with other people. A few years back, in the summer of 2011, I became inspired to do what my parents suggested. I recalled my personal experiences and memoirs, history lessons learned attending schools, and the countless valuable messages conceived from my parents writing this text. Truly, this book is a reflection of how they raised and taught me to "push on" even when I was too tired and weary from the trials and tribulations life offers.

I also would like to thank my former professors, Dr. Russell Adams, Dr. Valerie Janesick, Dr. Mike Maly, and so many others who inspired and taught me the value of teaching and learning. Their words and advice continue to speak to me as I teach college students. More important, I cannot forget the numerous change agents fighting to make our world and society a better place. Their readings, books, speeches, and videos radicalized the way I view the world while, at the same time, motivating me to continue to remain in this field working with youth.

I have the highest praise for the children I teach every day who inspire me more than they will ever know. They take me back to a time when I was a struggling student searching desperately to find myself and fulfill a dream seemingly distant, yet so close. I especially love the way they continue to journey through education, not giving up on the hope for a better tomorrow.

Lastly, I cannot forget about my beautiful family, wife, kids, aunts, cousins, and other kinfolk who mean so much to me as I try to represent what our ancestors wished for us to accomplish in this "short" life the creator grants. Their love, admiration, and support empower me.

INTRODUCTION

More than twenty-five years ago I saw myself happily teaching history to young people in a school I cherished and loved. Not only was I a powerful stakeholder in the community where I taught, lived, and raised my children, but my kids attended the school where I tirelessly worked besides my colleagues to improve our curriculum and cultural environment.

A lot has changed in my life since becoming a teacher, a profession I used to feel very proud and excited to be part of. Today, I no longer share this opinion and believe my role in education is becoming extinct, along with my methods.

Schools have been around for a long time before ancient Egyptians walked the earth. Education started in the home, later transcending from family-managed systems into school communities. Where people prayed and lived determined the type of education and schooling children experienced. In some countries, methods are one hundred years old and have not changed to satisfy European cultural imperialist or hegemonic beliefs.

Besides technology's impact on schooling, many nations outside the United States apply similar methods their grandparents were taught and recycle traditional habits, rituals, and knowledge to their offspring (Achebe 2009). It is no coincidence that when some foreigners visit countries like the United States with these backgrounds they perform admirably in American schools. Their longstanding history, involvement, and development in education makes it possible for them to go anywhere in the world to achieve high academic results.

There is a lot to say about today's public schools situated in urban communities, especially when dealing with teaching African American children. As a proud African American male, I have great memories of growing up in a community of esteemed African American and white American educators helping me develop. I experienced school leaders, teachers, and coaches working alongside one another with my parents to ensure my intellectual capital would thrive. A good number of educators taught me how to read, do math, write, and learn powerful history lessons that remain with me to this day.

American educators play an important part in bringing up African Americans in this nation's history. Besides the clergy or black churches, teachers have been the most important figures in African American lives. Teachers have taught us valuable lessons, including how to advocate for each other and our communities, and they helped us develop critical academic skills so we can earn enough to take care of our families. Some schools tried to teach us how to love and appreciate other cultures. During my primary school years, quite a few teachers read Jessie Jackson's sermon, "I am somebody," as we sang, "Lift Every Voice and Sing" alongside the Pledge of Allegiance.

Without teachers or schools, many people's lives would be lost. Our parents made a huge difference with the way schools were run because they were stakeholders. They worked with the teachers to ensure our success. When we got into trouble in school, the teachers called our parents to inform them of the disciplinary policies or practices they agreed upon to correct or check behavior. Of course my parents wanted my booty spanked, so that's what happened. Today, corporal punishment is frowned upon and rarely occurs.

As my parents believed, with countless other African American families, it was better for a teacher versus a police officer to check unacceptable behavior. Teachers, parents, and students negotiated and agreed to best practices that made schools special and unique. This is not to say such a belief or practice no longer exists; however, so much has changed with the way schools operate and educate students.

I'm afraid education has lost its zeal and former structure that once made it an idea profession. The best schools operating today exist in strong communities where parents, as stakeholders, collaborate with teachers to raise the future of this nation. A lot can be said with what is happening within the inner workings of these school environments, especially when it comes down to teaching practices and methods used to help students achieve high results. Why can't similar practices once again occur in urban America, with people saying what students learn and how they apply their education?

This book is an appeal to parents, teachers, and policymakers alike to challenge the notion of how schools are managed and run in many communities throughout America. In particular, it unlike districts that have resources, strong families, and effective parental input, many schools lacking these assets remain the most vulnerable for reform. Take for example districts such as Naperville, Wheaton, and Glenbard in Illinois Dupage county where resources are viable to schools and parents have a strong say in the direction of the school district.

From my lens, such reform is seemingly more capitalistic in nature than transformative. There is a lot of money to be made in education, a once untapped market. No one argues that change is unnecessary or unneeded in order to correct poor schooling practices or that past methods can't be improved upon. However, who should have a say about what goes on with schools does matter. Excluding parents, communities, and minorities from school reform does not make it about them but about the people with the power and money to control how they think schools should function.

If African American parents or teachers who look like the children being educated in reformed schools have limited say, then what is society really saying about the way these "good faith" people or corporate philanthropists really think and feel about those people? How can you say you love the children but do not want to hear from and instead ignore the parents or people who are ethnically similar?

The book is comprised of five parts. Part 1, Upbringing, deals with my reasons for becoming an educator. It also provides the origins of community school practices and the positive ways it educated people in this nation's history. In addition, best educational practices and methods are reviewed.

Part 2, Reality, discusses the challenges I experienced in education, which dissolved my ostensible naïveté in this profession. Furthermore, I review some of the pitfalls and challenges I learned after three years in the profession.

Part 3, It's the Journey, explains the cultural practices and instructional tools used in education to engage and connect with students. Culturally relevant education is discussed greatly in this section as I unravel the usefulness of the theories and applied approaches to educating minority students.

Part 4, Can you Stand the Rain?, examines the challenges of school reform experienced as a teacher and the drawbacks, consequences, and racial undertones associated with school closures. The section further discusses my exodus from administration, believing it impossible to lead in the present school climate.

Finally, part 5, How Freedom Schools Help Educators Navigate School Reform, reviews the pros of school reform through the eyes of emergent schooling practices of freedom schools. Freedom schools were the original premise or foundation for community schooling efforts in this nation's past and remain a viable option for parents and teachers seeking change.

PART I

Upbringing

Perspective

For years, the public school system has been replete with examples of high-performing structures that worked to empower the achievement for students across America. Since the conception of the Midwest Northwest Ordinance Act of 1787, education has been a cornerstone for raising people out of poverty (Shujaa 1994). Many minorities and immigrants were able to acquire specific skills that provided them with greater access to the capitalist system.

A considerable number of schools prior to the Northwest Ordinance Act initially only served the interest of the elite; however, over time, with larger white immigrant groups from Eastern Europe settling into urban areas of the northeast, the notion of public schooling began take hold and prepare new Americans for the workforce. In addition, a concern similar to the crisis dealing with recently freed blacks was that young minorities had to become disciplined to improve their assimilation into the American landscape.

Specific questions arose during the early 1900s, when many immigrant children were exploited in America's industrial agency and were denied access to schooling. The theory went: if minority children could go to work in highly dangerous environments to tackle arduous tasks, why were they not in school to go beyond the factory model? So many young people were exploited and injured completing jobs around factories that child labor laws were eventually passed to prohibit such employment. With young children no longer able to work in the factories, where would they go? School became the only viable choice.

During the Reconstruction Era, after the Civil War, the country was gripped with one abiding question: what shall we do with the Negro? The government established "freedom schools," as some African Americans called it, and these were the first precepts to manifest the nation's ideal of democracy toward people they'd held in bondage for years (Anderson 1988). Regardless of the intent, good or bad, African Americans young and old flocked to these schools to learn how to read and write, skills that once were prohibited and seen as a crime during chattel slavery. Freedom Schools not only served African Americans but also poor rural whites who did not have access to educational opportunities in the South.

During the Reconstruction Era, a large burgeoning class of American men and women appeared on the scene to compete in the economy. African Americans improving their status in the country ultimately threatened the white status quo, which saw them as less important or inferior; furthermore, this notion was used to cover up the fact that whites would have to compete against blacks for jobs in the new South. As a result, disenfranchisement and other oppressive laws were legislated to deny blacks equal access in America's social, political, and economic landscape.

From the Black Codes (laws with the intent and effect of restricting African Americans' freedom and of compelling them to work in a labor economy based on low wages or debt) and Slaughter-House Cases of 1873 (the first US Supreme Court interpretation of the recently enacted Fourteenth Amendment to the Constitution), to poll tax and *Plessy v. Ferguson* (a landmark US Supreme Court decision upholding the constitutionality of state laws requiring racial segregation in public facilities under the doctrine of "separate but equal"), African Americans were being subjected to a cruel legal and policy fate that would strip them of the gains they had made during the Reconstruction Era. One of the most difficult hurdles African Americans would encounter from these new discriminatory practices dealt with having access to a quality public education. In fact, today's African Americans continue to encounter the same challenge of acquiring an equitable education.

During the Reconstruction and post-Reconstruction eras, African American universities and college systems emerged to offset the nation's new racial policies. The spirit of white philanthropy, radical counterhegemony, and assimilation beliefs gave rise to the concept of African American college schooling. Philanthropists designed universities specifically for African Americans to enforce two major concepts: Jim Crow laws (state and local laws that enforced racial segregation in the Southern United States) and the training of a new African American intellectual class that could assimilate and guide the race. It is no coincidence that most black colleges exist in the South, which supported the notion of segregated schooling practices.

More important, Booker T. Washington cannot be left out of this conversation. His due diligence and efforts helped bring forth many of these educational models in the South. With the support of his mentor and financier, Samuel Chapman, founder of Hampton University, Washington was able to raise the funds and resources and establish a network that helped him create Tuskegee University. As a result of Booker T. Washington's radical and successful attempt to establish a college for African Americans that trained and prepared them vocationally, his idea of educational and social advancement was promoted throughout the South (Carroll 2006).

Not only did many white philanthropists feel a quintessential need to help train and prepare African Americans to work in the economy, they believed it would enforce an autonomous community that could exist outside the periphery of white society. African American churches, along with Washington's efforts, were able to engineer universities and colleges throughout the South, along with the support of white humanitarianism, which developed independent schooling. As a result, many African Americans became trained and skilled in professions that advanced their communities. One cannot forget that many African Americans came with an innate, specific set of skills from chattel slavery that built the South's economy and much of colonial America. Now these same skills would establish institutions. Not surprisingly, self-sufficient, prosperous towns and schools emerged for African Americans in the southern and western parts of this nation.

In further support of the new South's racial policies, public schools that catered to African Americans were underfunded and poorly staffed. Whether independent or public, many African American schools during the post-Reconstruction years struggled to survive because they could not rely on white support or public resources. As a result, a great many of these schools lacked books and supplies. Moreover, a great deal of educators did not have college training, so students quite often relied on teachers with an eighth- to twelfth-grade education. This did not take away from the fact that students received the best education the system offered.

Another dilemma that impacted African American schooling was that of the economy. A great deal of African Americans remained sharecroppers in the rural Deep South; consequently, when harvest time emerged, all hands were on deck, which meant that most of the children had to leave their schooling to help the community. As a result, from the 1900s to the 1930s, a considerable number of African American children who lived in the South were forced to stop their schooling early (Anderson 1988). Notwithstanding, children who were afforded the opportunity to acquire a public education did quite well in the American economy and worked to improve their class status.

A new class of African Americans emerged as a result of their experiences in public education and college. W. E. B. Du Bois publicized this new group as "the talented tenth" (Du Bois 1903).

African Americans who advanced themselves through schooling established a newfound sense of synergy that empowered them to become civil leaders, educators, scholars, and intellectuals of their community and society. Organizations sprang forth that not only tackled the race problem but sought to change the policies that oppressed their communities. From the Niagara Fall Movement that later became known as the NAACP, progressive whites, Jews, and African Americans helped develop organizations to democratize the nation to turn away from harmful practices. This new class of African Americans established banks, insurance companies, grocery stores, schools, and hotels. Access to a public education, despite its limitations, helped to provide an education that taught people how to provide for themselves. Without question, the social and political policies at the time also made African Americans realize that they needed to support each other to survive, defend against, and insulate themselves from the attacks of racism. Throughout the years of public schooling, an important concept remains: the opportunity and ability to access a fair, equitable education helps progress African Americans' status in America.

Ambitions

Growing up, I always felt the need to communicate to people my concerns or views on any given topic. You may call it "the gift of gab." Others may view it as a need to be heard. My loving mother always felt I should pursue the field of law since I always had a comment or rebuttal to dispute her wishes around the house. Mainly, though, I believed I had some sort of special way of voicing my perspective. Instead of becoming a lawyer or a gifted motivational speaker like Les Brown, I decided to enter the teaching profession. Here is where I believed I could really make a difference that not only supported my community but helped guide or shape the thinking of young people. My first desire to become an educator became rooted in me as a junior-year undergrad at Howard University. I was sincerely influenced by the brightest minds of professors, such as my African American history professor, Dr. Adams, who shaped my worldview of politics, race, sociology, and economics. He helped me identify a sense of purpose for teaching because I envisioned that I could possibly change humanity. Idealistic or not, I believed I could make a huge difference in the communities or nation in which I lived.

For years I had always been impressed with the way teachers were able to influence students—not just because they were able to regurgitate certain facts, whether boring or not—but their dedication and commitment to teaching and learning seemed real. Yes, I have had some poor teachers, just as I have experienced poor mechanics, salespeople, physicians, and fix-it staff.

But what excited me about entering the teaching profession was that for the most part, educators harbored an ethno-humanist facet or interpersonal human connection to people that allowed them to change the way people felt about an issue. An effective or quality teacher could make a connection to a certain subject and help students learn how to dissect and interpret its meaning. In doing so, students could understand the real meaning behind the taught view; more importantly, they could internalize the message the teacher tried to communicate.

I believe here is where I discovered my greatest professional passion. While at Howard University, people would inquire about my major. At first I didn't know. Maybe business management or accounting because this is where the money is? How about some type of technical field like computer science or engineering? But when I really begin to learn the beauty of seeking knowledge and the joy that it brought to my mind, I found my calling here.

When I told my parents and friends what I wanted to do, they did a double take and stated, "Teaching? Why teaching? You're not going to make any money."

True, but I would enjoy the ability to communicate information to kids that will empower them. But as my father declared, "An idealist is someone who thinks he can change the world, so good luck with that."

In fact, my father wanted me to study business management to learn how to organize and develop a business while making some money. At the time, he had a small business in Chicago that had a city contract with Chicago public schools and the Chicago Transit Authority. He believed, like most of my friends' parents, that idealism or changing the world had died out in the '60s. Today, in America, it's about making some "paper" to take care of your family to live a quality life. In many ways, I believed my father was scared for me because he felt I would surely struggle trying to earn a decent wage in education. Also, how many of these children would I truly be able to salvage or change?

However, my calling was clear, and nothing would stop me from joining the professional community of educators. When I declared my major as an educator and studied history to "learn the truth," little did I know what awaited me.

Several professors of mine were excited about my educational journey. I must admit that my parents were happy for me, because they could truly see that I enjoyed my major, plus I made good grades. More importantly, I would be able to find work because there were simply not a lot of black males in education.

Yet I also have to be honest and tell you that there were a couple of professors who attempted to discourage me from following this profession. They felt that teachers were underappreciated and viewed as "slouches." As one of my professors told me, "Not too many people respect the work we do." I have often heard the phrase that anybody can be a teacher. How about this statement? "Teachers teach while others actually do." More importantly, my professor said she had to work two jobs just to make ends meet. Here was a brilliant woman with a PhD telling me she could not afford to live off her professor salary alone. Not to mention the fact that she believed most people did not appreciate her professional skills. Surely this was something to ponder entering the field. I guess for me, at the time, I felt strongly about making a difference over earning a whole lot of money.

Growing up, I had two professional parents, so you could say I was a middle-class person. My father had an engineering degree from Purdue University and worked for Standard Oil for twenty years before starting his own business. My mom worked at the Environmental Protection Agency and had a degree in public relations. Both drove home the value of receiving an education to my sister and me. School was taken seriously in our home, and I was always taught that an education could take you far in life. As a result, I knew the importance of an education and valued how it could change or impact my life.

As a child, I have to admit I got what I wanted. I had every toy, video game, and gym shoe I wanted and believed I was entitled. My parents spoiled me. Now I was entering a profession where I could afford not Nikes but rather Payless brand shoes. This drove me to stay in school beyond my undergraduate years because I figured my earning potential would increase with years of education. Also, unlike my college professor, I would not mind working a second job, maybe as a part-time college instructor or a summer school teacher, to earn a few bucks here or there. Whatever the case, my heart was set on becoming a teacher. The way I saw it, people have to invest in a career they enjoy. As my father once stated, "Whatever gets you out of bed in the morning is what you want to do for the rest of your life." When a person truly loves a thing, it compels him or her to pursue it to the end no matter what happens. Teaching, here I come.

Upon receiving my undergraduate degree in education/history, I received my first job as an instructor at an alternative high school in Chicago.

All I remember the principal saying when she first saw me was, "You're hired."

I thought, *Great, I get to move out of my parents' house and begin my new life.*

The trouble was, I really didn't understand what awaited me, but I felt prepared to take on this new job. Hell, I had the education and credentials. I was working toward my master's degree in education and history starting that fall. Also, this was a school for students who did not succeed in a traditional educational model and required a new direction or alternative to learning. I thought, I could do this job.

The only thing the principal gave me was a key to my room, a copy of the teacher's edition or course text with coded answer keys and the publisher's annotated notes, and the school's policy handbook. I received the history's department curriculum, a course outline, and content on ethics all in the same day. I thought, *Where is the teacher's lounge? And what day did you say we started school?*

9

The real truth of that matter is I probably should have been given the history of the school's curriculum or a course outline, but there was none. I should have been assigned a mentor, with his or her contact information so I could start meeting with him or her right away. Also, as not to put all the blame on my principal, I should have researched the school a bit more before taking the first job offered to me.

As a Matter of Fact

A good deal of first-year teachers enter the system with the hopes of changing the minds and hearts of children. Despite the often-negative cynicism thrust toward teachers concerning why they enter the field of education—from having summers off to working shorter days to low accountability—educators invest in the value of the human spirit. Although this may sound a bit "cheesy" or too convoluted, the fact remains that the teaching profession usually attracts people who believe they can make a difference or have a positive impact on children. Considerable amounts of research and qualitative interviews of first-year teachers reveal this fact (Kozol 2012).

Not to mention, educators invested in the profession spend a considerable amount of time outside their six- to eight-hour school workday. Successful teachers spend a great amount of time managing and reviewing the curriculum; researching and developing informative, content-worthy lessons that align to state standards; and correctly assessing the performance of their students.

However, the most important part of being an effective teacher deals with the ability to make proper connections to students. Enough data supports this notion, because when properly connecting with students from a interpersonal perspective, they discovered the relevance of the educator and the point of learning the lesson (Billings 1996). Simply put, successful teaching requires the ability to connect with the students while making the curriculum relevant to them.

Dr. Wong (2009), in his well-known book *First Days of School: How to Be an Effective Teacher*, thoroughly examines this concept in his research. From his perspective, successful educators "must have" their content or curriculum mastered. Not thoroughly knowing the subject makes the educator unprepared to teach. The first rule of thumb for an educator is to learn the subject areas inside and out. Quite honestly, this does not always occur during the first year of teaching. This consumes the teacher his or her entire career, which makes the statement "a lifelong learner" a fact for the educator. Countless educators continue not only learning their subject area to become more effective professionals, but they return to school to learn more effective strategies and pertinent skills.

A second critical point Dr. Wong expresses is a teacher's ability to prepare his or her curriculum two to three months in advance, before entering the classroom. Of course, this a difficult task for a first-year educator, because the truth of the matter is, many such teachers are just leaving college and have yet to prepare or been informed about their new school's pedagogical practice (teaching methods).

Today, many school districts take the initiative to train their first-year teachers in workshop forums about their curriculum and what these teachers must apply to achieve a quality evaluation and high performance rating. In the summer months after school has let out, these same teachers come to their newly assigned schools two to three times weekly—often for free—to study the curriculum to prepare their future lessons. This takes a considerable amount of time and effort from the first-year educator, which helps them to understand the seriousness and expectation of their profession. Not to the mention the fact that to plan a successful curriculum really takes a great deal of time and patience. Of course, a teacher's plans must be tested on his or her subjects, the students. If the plans fail, well, quite honestly, a teacher must start over to retry a new strategy to successfully achieve the lesson's objective.

Many first-year teachers struggle with this concept, not understanding that every lesson will not be automatically robotic or magical without first having the opportunity to teach it to students. A lesson may go well at first for a successful veteran teacher for one class, but another class will struggle with the lesson's strategy; therefore, the teacher may have to reconfigure the strategy for a different set of students or to another class with similar dynamics. In other words, what works well for one group of students may not work very well for another set of learners. As a result, during the course of their school day, effective teachers usually adjust their lessons to accommodate the needs of students. Only when a teacher learns his or her class and understands the students within that environment will the teacher be able to create quality lessons.

Another argument that Wong makes regarding effective teaching deals with becoming an effective manager in the classroom. Successful teaching does not rest with the concept that students need to be transformed into a future Einstein or US president; rather, it is based on the ability of a teacher to help students achieve the expectations of their learning environment. Another way of saying this is that rules and criteria are important for kids to apply in order to reach some level of success.

The majority of successful industries or businesses apply a set of standards or expectations they expect their employees to practice to achieve quality results. This is no different from teaching students. Teachers who become effective managers eventually empower students to learn academic lessons within cooperative learning groups and tiered arrangements rather than mostly apply a direct teaching methodology.

Today, educators have coined the phrase "master teacher," which means a successful teacher who does not use a direct instructional methodology but creates a learning environment that is student-centered. This means the instructor develops and enriches the curriculum to the point where students take control of their own learning. Now, let's be clear; there are not a whole lot of educators entering their first year of teaching as master instructors. It's a long, demanding journey to reach this point as an educator. Through experience and time, effective educators learn how to adapt their lessons to meet the needs of their students. When a teacher successfully manages the classroom, this increases his or her potential to apply a facilitative teaching model. Again, to have an engaged, student-centered approach in the classroom, a teacher must be an effective manager.

What does a manager need to do to be successful in the classroom? According to Wong, establishing routines and procedures help students apply the classroom norms of a learning environment. When dealing with routines and procedures, it's important for students to know upon entering the classroom what is expected of them. What's the first thing students will do when they enter the classroom? Talk to their friends and wait for the teacher to start the lesson, or begin right away with a bell-ringer or warm-up exercise. Of course, the latter is necessary while the teacher takes attendance and directs students' focus to complete the task.

Another important quality that deals with routines and procedures is the teacher's ability to have an itinerary or classroom goals so the class knows what is expected of them. After review of the warm-up lesson, it is important for a teacher to know the requirements the class will complete for that day; afterward, this is where the real test of an effective lesson begins. A bigger question that effective teachers always have to answer is: Will this lesson engage students? If so, much of the research suggests engaging lessons reduces disciplinary or behavior problems in a classroom (Billings 2009). Teachers who design an engaging lesson are not only skilled at differentiating the lesson to meet the learning needs of their students but are able to modify instructions to achieve the learning goal. Again, this takes time and experience, which a first-year teacher will struggle with.

Today, many first-year teachers are assigned mentors by their schools to help them understand how to apply effective lessons to their classes. Additionally, mentors help these instructors problem solve and strategize how to improve their lessons and connect with students. Perhaps most importantly, essential instructors establish a set of classroom norms that align with a school's policy to achieve a productive learning environment. These norms are made clear to students everyday in the classroom. When students abide by and adhere to the classroom's expectations, it increases their ability to become successful learners.

However, when teachers have to constantly battle students, it leads to unsuccessful instruction, because learners are not achieving the expectations of the classroom. Maintaining high expectations in a classroom is important for every effective teacher to succeed. If teachers have low expectations about their students or classrooms, it is reflected in their instruction and how students react.

Another great conversation behind what makes an effective teacher deals with their ability to relate and connect with their students. Now, this does not mean becoming their friend; however, it suggests quality teaching and learning are most effective when the subject matter connects with students. In many ways, the lesson has to connect to the language, culture, and relevancy of the student. This is not to suggest that every lesson that does not meet this set of expectations is a poor lesson, especially in the fields of math and science. What it does argue is that when lessons are able to connect to students, their engaging with the subject becomes more invested. To develop a relevant, engaging lesson everyday in a classroom is not easy and takes a great deal of preparation and skill development. It is especially no easy task for first-year teachers who struggle with just learning the curriculum and their students. However, schools assigning mentors and districts offering professional development sessions only increase their potential to create engaging and relevant lessons.

In addition, it is important that teachers learn their students. This is what makes the first five weeks of schools so critical to any teacher with a new set of learners in front of them. Just learning their names is not enough to build connections. A personal investment has to take place for a teacher to be able to build a classroom connection to students (Billings 2006). As often the case, getting to know someone takes time. Within those five weeks it is critical for teachers to learn an important characteristic or personal interest of the student to begin building that connection. From calling home to check on a troubled or absent student, to praising and recognizing students for their accomplishment or efforts, to learning the students' hobbies or life goals, these are necessary actions that ultimately help build a well-connected, caring, and quality classroom environment. From the onset, an outsider visiting a teacher's classroom can tell whether productive teaching is taking place. A classroom climate has a lot to do with producing quality results and effective learning.

So here we are: to become a quality, effective teacher takes experience, patience, and a whole lot of practice. It is no easy task to achieve, nor is it an easy job to assume just because a teacher gets summers off. Unquestionably, what makes an effective teacher deals with his or her ability to master the curriculum and their subject area; plan effective, relevant lessons; become quality managers in the classroom to ensure learning is taking place; and become sort of a personal coach who works to build a connection with students. All of these require a great deal of skill training and effort. Most importantly, these are the important skills and traits all new teachers will have to learn to succeed.

The Making of You

My first year of teaching took a whole lot of radical adjustments to survive in the classroom. I especially did not mind learning new strategies to effectively teach; the only problem was that I had to learn most of this on my own. Please don't get me wrong. I had a considerable amount of support and assistance from my principal, but I struggled without a mentor or veteran helping me sort out the various ways I could make my curriculum more effective.

Take for instance the concept of remapping the curriculum. In my possession were the state curriculum goals and indicators, along with the state's teacher textbook, yet much of what I prepared was subjective, or what I believed students needed to know. In the end, teaching content versus skill was my major concern.

A lot has changed in education today because university education programs teach the reverse: skill over content, which supports the teachers' ability to increase the students' proficiency and performance in reading, writing, math, and problem solving. However, at this particular time, I believed it was important to make sure students not only knew about the causes and effects of the American Revolutionary War but how the battles were won and the Masonic heritage of the Founding Fathers. Of course this made the conversations and content with students more engaging and interesting, yet I was focused on testing their review of this information versus the skills they were supposed to gain studying the subject.

Another interesting lesson I had to learn my first year was, despite how much you loved the subject, it did not mean the students cared about it at all. In fact, some were bold enough to tell you to your face your subject stinks. This was where I had to learn effective strategies and interesting ways to teach the subject besides just lecturing a whole lot of content. As a result, the first three months of my professional life were challenging because I worked incredibly hard trying to figure out how to make the lessons relevant and noteworthy.

Activities teachers today call "jigsaw," "carousel," "share-pair," "storyboard," "map quest," "menu options," and countless others all refer to cooperative learning activities that help students engage in a classroom. I would start with one strategy and build on that for a couple of months, twisting and reconfiguring its arrangements and techniques, while researching and pursuing new leads from teachers as to how I should further improve my subject. Although the students, colleagues, and the principal applauded my efforts, no one told me I would have to work so hard just to develop a lesson. During my first six months, I was married to the curriculum, the subject, and the school. Dedication, hard work, and commitment are what I found most teachers apply to educate students. The veteran teachers who were at it a little longer had more experience and treasures to extract from to help support their practice. Similar to what was mentioned earlier from Dr. Wong (that an effective educator must master his or her content or know it thoroughly), I can say it took me about two to three years in my subject area to get the basics down of the content. But that first year, before I could provide the students with an assignment, I had to study it, prepare notes, and research other important aspects of the content. This took a great deal of time, which meant my social life during the school year suffered. At this point, I believed I was just surviving, doing the best I could with the curriculum.

Did I mention that I worked at an alternative high school? One very important thing I learned my first year was that connections are important the first couple of weeks of school. Before I started teaching, I should have used that time to learn something about my students. This entailed getting the roster before school began to discover some fascinating things about them. Also, interviewing former teachers, counselors, or administrators would have greatly helped me learn a little more about them. This is not saying teachers should judge students before they enter their classrooms; on the other hand, having a profile or background information is very helpful because this allows teachers to plan ahead while working out the arrangements of their classroom. It further helps the teacher become more aware of the challenged learners who will eventually appear in their room. Having this information, the teacher can contact the student and parents before school begins to introduce him or herself to discuss their plans, goals, and expectations for the upcoming academic year.

With all this being said, I only spent two days learning student names while hardly doing any warm-up or interpersonal activities. As a result, I really didn't know who was in my classroom that first month, and I struggled with knowing what their interests were, who should become a peer buddy or instructional partner, or better yet, how I should have arranged my seating chart. When I finally did my seating chart and had my room set up in a particular way, I soon realized how awkward it was that I did not plan ahead to know my students.

Building connections with students does not just involve knowing their first name but knowing where they came from, the skill sets they bring with them, the prior knowledge they harbor, and personal interests and goals outside your room. One thing I had working for me was that I could relate to many of my students' cultural idioms, and diatribes, which helped me gain their confidence, appreciation, and support.

This would not have lasted if I didn't work my butt off to prove that I cared about their learning. Despite my having the same cultural ethos of my students, this is no way suggests teachers from a varied or different ethnicity could not do the same. In fact, whenever a person experiences a different culture or heritage, it is most useful to study certain characteristics that compose that group. It does mean a person has to pretend as though he or she has the same experiences or backgrounds as the students. This was not the case with me, but having the ability to learn, relate to, and connect with their heritage helps make the educator more authentic.

Despite some of the profanity, arguments, misunderstandings, fighting, and dispirited attitudes I encountered daily at my new school, I was able to get to know my students' idiosyncrasies, which helped me build a connection. This is true for any educator.

When all was said and done, I survived my first year of teaching. What I remember most about my first year was how tired I was after work. The first thing I would do at home was take a nap. The school and students sucked my energy dry during the day.

My commitment to them and my quest to succeed equipped me with more treasures that I could not have possibly gained working anywhere else. This was not only an incredible, rewarding field of study but also a challenged profession that took a whole lot of effort to achieve. In the end, I was not able to reach all students that I encountered, nor was I able to increase everyone's interest in history. But what I was able to do was help make my subject come to life. I believe this is my most powerful educational strength and asset to teaching, which continues to make me enjoy working with students. What I also took from my first year was the importance of establishing a connection to students before the year begins, not after. Learning about the students, researching their interest, and interviewing former teachers and other important figures are very important to help establish a connective relationship. School does not just begin on the first day of study; it lasts a lifetime.

As I continued my own studies to advance my education, I also learned that the most important research I conducted was with my own students. They taught me more in one year than I could have ever learned studying at a college. Yes, my teaching practicum was good experience, and the courses' content and skill-based training was specific and concrete; however, nothing compared to learning more about my profession than interacting with students. After all, this is what makes most educators commit to our profession, because it's what makes us teachers.

Teaching Is an Art Form

Teachers with years of experience and techniques are more equipped to instruct any kind of student. Constant practice at the craft; the usage of repetitive routines in the classroom; a personalized managerial style of leadership; the application of providing equity to students in the classroom; and the ability to master one's content make for a quality instructor. Of course, there are other examples that can be duly noted about what characteristics apply to a quality instructor, but what becomes clear is that without practice, routines, research, personality, and knowledge of content that extends beyond the curriculum, a teacher will struggle.

Some researchers argue that it takes about six years to become a quality instructor, not the three-years limit prescribed by districts to determine tenure (Sergionvanni 1996).

Others suggest gaining mastery of the teaching profession occurs between two and three years, yet it depends on the educator's ability to

(1) quickly learn the profession while consistently researching their content;

(2) participate in skill-based seminars or continued education programs; or

(3) apply the techniques demonstrated to them from a mentor (Delpit 2013).

It is clear that without the necessary support; consistent application of learned concepts; and a strong commitment to the profession, a new teacher will not last very long. In fact, according to Wong (2009), after six years, roughly about 32 percent of classroom instructors take flight from teaching or choose another profession.

The great thing about wanting to improve in education deals with the amount of passion a teacher possesses. Typically, an instructor provided with great administrative and mentor support exists within a productive school climate and culture and has professional resources at their disposal. Most importantly, what makes a teacher most successful is the ability to practice his or her craft as an art form.

A professional dancer can spend anywhere from two to four hours a day crafting techniques and skills after rehearsal or practice. It is not just that the dancer has already practiced the routines that will make him or her unique, but also the ability to continue this regiment after the scheduled time to help achieve the desired performance skill. The stretching of muscles—the ability to make extra usage of leg tendons after long hours of excruciating practice and the focus and commitment it takes to master necessary moves—relates to what it takes for a teacher to be effective. The long hours a typical teacher expends after school deals with him or her reviewing and reflecting on the lesson; the assessment and skill review of the learners; the design or retooling it takes to prepare for the next day's instruction; and the constant study or research of the subject to make it relevant equates itself with being a professional dancer (Janesick 2010).

Teachers and professional artists or performers have a great deal in common, which is their ability to consistently work long hours after their performance. To succeed in anything takes a great deal of practice and commitment. Take for example George "Iceman" Gervin's work ethic of learning how to shoot. Gervin is an American Basketball Association (ABA) and National Basketball Association (NBA) Hall of Famer. While growing up, he said that before he went home at night, he committed to making one hundred consecutive free throw shots. If he happened to get to the ninety-ninth free throw and miss, he would start all over again until he made one hundred straight shots (www.nba.com/history/players/ gervin_bio.html). This incredible story details the level of commitment it takes for a basketball player to be successful no matter how great his or her skill level; moreover, it is reflected in the amount of time and energy it takes for a teacher to become successful. Lots of practice, consistent routines, a conscious effort to always improve upon the lesson, and an abiding commitment to help learners achieve the instructional objective are what make for a quality teacher.

It can also be duly noted that sometime the best of us fail to achieve the desired outcome, or we come up short. Michael Jordan, arguably the greatest player to ever play the game of basketball, communicated in a famous Nike commercial that, "I've missed more than nine thousand shots in my career. I've lost almost three hundred games. Twenty-six times I've been trusted to take the game winning shot and missed. I've failed over and over and over again in my life. And that is why I succeed" (Smith 2014).

This is most notable because when we relate this to the teaching profession, we realize every lesson will not be great. Some lessons will not succeed in reaching every student in the classroom, and more important, not all lessons will be engaging instructional activities. Such a disappointment should cause an instructor to review his or her lessons to make necessary adjustments. The letdown for students is when teacher does not make the necessary modifications, which reduces the potency of the learning objective and makes whatever lesson the teacher is trying to teach less important to students. When Michael Jordan recognized his shortcomings, he practiced hard until he improved his craft (Smith 2014). When educators are provided the right type of support, provided constructive professional feedback, and allowed to learn from their mistakes, they are effective teachers.

However, today's climate of teaching does not allow educators to make too many mistakes in a classroom. Any shortcomings from an instructor are mostly viewed as their being a poor teacher, which eventually may result in his or her firing. This is not to say there are no ineffective teachers in the profession, yet too often teachers are heavily monitored or quickly dismissed for not mastering a district's curriculum.

What makes teaching like an art form is the fact that educators are constantly practicing their routines and subject areas long after students have left their classrooms. Similar to dancers or basketball players, it takes a considerable amount of patience and a strong work ethic to master a desired skill. Teachers are good at what they do when they recognize that reflection and modifying lessons help improve their instruction. Not to mention the fact that a typical teacher spends on average about ten hours a day working to assess students, prepare lessons, and research their subject (Defour and Eaker 1998).

Although some skeptics believe that teaching is only six hours worth of work, they are only viewing the daily performance of the instructor in the classroom. The planning, studying, and preparation by an effective instructor continues right up to the time he or she stands before the classroom. A good teacher is always thinking about teaching and learning, focused on how to make the instructions relevant and engaging. Also, teachers are dedicated to working on their skills to improve their effectiveness in the classroom. Quite often, most teachers return to school or seek professional development training to help them improve. Today's teachers in America are the most educated workforce or group of professionals (Douglass and Crowson 2011).

Despite the scrutiny of educators from policymakers, politicians, and businesspeople, teachers are focused on improving their craft.

Growing Pains

Years two and three as a teacher were much better for me as I committed myself to learn from my first year. Although I still had no mentor and needed to further develop the curriculum, I researched or reviewed other school's history departments to determine how they successfully targeted and aligned their instruction to the state's goals. More importantly, this time around I refused to be caught off guard because I failed to inquire about potential incoming students. Before the first school year ended, I was able to acquire my schedule and roster for the upcoming academic year. With the exception of transfer students, I was able to interview professional members at my school to obtain a pretty good profile of my future students. During this timeframe, I was constantly studying new teaching strategies to improve the engagement and achievement of the learners.

However, I believe my true shortcoming with teaching laid with my inability to focus on skill over content. Actually, I was not even conscious of such terminology at the time of my teaching, because I believed by students learning content, it helped them to obtain critical reading and writing skills they required to succeed beyond high school. Also, I found it to be a bit tough trying to avoid school politics, which at times appeared worst than the politics on Capitol Hill.

When the school year began, my classroom was ready, my curriculum for the first semester was solid, and my instructional strategies were expanding and improving. The only thing I felt I needed to concentrate on was targeting those learners who came with some behavioral and academic challenges. This was where their profiles helped add to the strength of my teaching but also problem solved challenges that appeared in the classroom. Teaching in an alternative structure brought a unique set of challenges, because most of the students were far below grade level. As a result of my teaching at the sophomore level, most students were often older and fed up with school. Quite simply, it was our job to help them relearn how to enjoy school while helping them transition into a junior college or vocational program. If these students were able to obtain the types of academic skills necessary to succeed at a four-year college, our school community encouraged and helped them achieve this pursuit.

I began to view teaching as sort of a persuasive tool to convince students why they needed to learn this subject. I had to make the lesson as relevant as possible to help them build a connection with the subject; otherwise, they would not value the lesson or the class. When this occurred my first year, behavioral challenges emerged. To limit such activity, I made use of new and old teaching strategies, such as cooperative learning strategies, to reach and engage students. My tool chest as an instructor was building, and I could see the effects on my students.

Despite my best efforts to reach all my students, some were neither moved nor persuaded to learn the subject. A couple of students would cut my class or leave the school building altogether to avoid learning history. Others would not participate in the activities or lessons I spent hours developing.

Instead of giving up on these students, I attempted to adjust the curriculum by modifying the work to help them succeed. I became immersed with trying to figure out how I could best support these learners. However, what I discovered was that the students I struggled with had problems throughout the school day. I could perform a magic trick and they wouldn't care, so something else was needed to assist them. At one point I thought about extending myself professionally to offer a mentor or tutorial program to these struggling students. Yet my being in school and starting a new family made it hard to find the extra time to support them. This was where I began to become discouraged as a teacher, because no matter how hard I tried, I could not successfully reach some students.

Another dilemma that perplexed my efforts teaching dealt with improving the academic abilities of my learners. Most of the students I taught read at about the fifth- or sixth-grade level. It was my job to not only encourage their investment into education but to improve their reading and writing levels. I felt that if I could help the students enjoy the curriculum, they would see the value of learning, which would improve their academic skills. From setting up literacy circles, rewriting parts of history, acting out stories, writing poetry, and developing plays, I saw that most of my students became radically invested in learning the subject.

During this time I also harbored the notion that it was important to start where the students were. In other words, if they came to class reading at a fifth-grade level, I started by assigning books or supplementary resources that helped improve their study of the subject while growing their skills. Since I could not expend any more time after school to assist the efforts of my students, I believed it was imperative I came bright and early to await students who required further assistance or support. This additionally helped me to work on students' reading and writing skill sets. Through my challenges, it became imperative to learn from them to advance my teaching. I also felt that if I could demonstrate to students that I cared about their learning, in return they would apply themselves to excel in the curriculum.

Working with limited resources and support furthered my frustration. Since we were an alternative school, we received minimal resources. Our principal did not have a big discretionary budget to pull from, so if we wanted to do anything extra to support our students, it depended on the ability to raise funds or to spend our own money. Quite a few of the supplementary resources that I utilized in the classrooms came from schools that discarded the materials or donated the items, or we simply borrowed from their inventory. It also helped that our principal created a partnership with the neighboring schools, which sometime helped us to access desired resources. I would visit elementary and high schools on my scavenger hunt in search of items to support my students, even sometimes going through a school's dumpster or trash cans to grab what I could possibly use. In fact, one school threw out a whole bunch of desk atlases along with the teacher's edition, which I quickly scooped and continue to make some use of today. It is amazing what one can find in the back of a school when the year comes to an end. In fact, most students were not perturbed or made to feel ashamed making use of another person's throwaways because they believed it would help them succeed.

At this time, a bigger issue for me became how to expose our students to external environments that would increase their learning opportunities. Often, the case in urban alternative schools is that most of the students come from disadvantaged backgrounds. The only exposure they have about what exists outside their community is through TV shows. To offset this, I believed it was essential to plan outings and activities that were aligned with the curriculum. Living in a city is great because quite often there are numerous opportunities and funded programs for field trips. Whenever there was an important piece of historical information I believed could further instructionally and environmentally expose our students, I planned an educational journey. What I found was that students became more excited and engrossed about learning the subject. Even if I could not take them, they would learn a way to visit the historical place or event. In my history class, we also took community tours navigating through historic sections of the south side of Chicago, such as the Bronzeville community, to help make the school curriculum come to life.

The one advantage I had working here was that quite simply, no one gave a damn, in the outside world, what we were doing with our alternative kids. As long as they were not on the streets during the school day and were learning something, anything, it was perceived as "all good." Not to the mention the fact that at this time of my career, "high stakes testing," or standardized tests, did not define how well you taught your course for the year. The school and principal not only participated and helped support my adventures to expose and teach our students, they encouraged the level of learning they believed was taking place. Now this is not to say we went on a trip every three months, but we did try to go on at least four school outings a year.

Like anything, problems and challenges will surface. Regardless of my efforts to work with my students to expose them to external learning environments, a creative instructional pedagogy, or work with them before school to help improve their academic level, politics came to play. Due to our school having some attendance issues, small enrollment, and a skeletal budget, some administrative heads downtown were considering whether we should remain open. Now the proof was in the pudding, as my grandmother would say, because our graduation rate was the best the city offered for an alternative high school. However, from their viewpoint, there was not enough data to support how well students performed upon graduating our high school. Most of our students who graduated went to a junior college program; another amount of our learners decided to enter the military or acquire vocational training; and others just quite simply graduated, were tired of school, and got a job.

Yet our school needed to prove this to the "big tops" downtown at the district office. Consequently, our school began to forward a qualitative survey to our alumni to check on their current status while developing a computer program through the counselor's office to quantify or keep a record of those attending college. But what I saw happening here soon would take effect everywhere across the American urban school landscape—more efficient, businesslike schools that deal with just the bottom line.

Although it was early in my career, it became enough for me to witness that education and politics were really one and the same; business, as I saw it at the time, dealt with budgets and money that were distributed to schools to assist their efforts to increase achievement. Our school did not require a lot of money to stay afloat, but it required the support of the educational community and local politicians to see the value of our structure.

Despite our efforts as teachers and administrators, our little schoolhouse would eventually come under siege. I could not help but think concerning my school reality: *When will they begin to use the "test" to determine my effectiveness in the classroom rather than a targeted review of students' skill sets?*

PART II

Reality

Disintegration

In America, public schools have traditionally worked to equip their students with the necessary skills to become employed. Whether students sought to further apply their skills in a post-secondary setting or vocational institution, the primary function of public education was to prepare them to earn a quality living. Although today's public schools have been accused of having problems with helping students reach a specific skill set to succeed in the American economy, historically, these institutions have enriched people with the most quintessential resource: reading, writing, and arithmetic. The usage of quality reading and writing skills enable learners to work in an industrial, business, or service provider section of the economy; whereas mastery of math skills promote students' ability to become employed in a medical or technical field. Overall, one can argue that public schooling in America has enhanced the majority of the people. However, some Americans are confronted with the crisis of acquiring quality academic skills to prepare for future employment opportunities.

For years, minority communities have made use of ingenious strategies such as, political activism, community partnering, and financial planning to advance their public education interest. With limited resources and underfunded schools, minorities simply used what they had to teach their children. Specifically within the African American community, years of segregation and harsh racial policies attempted to stymie their development of quality schools. Yet with persistent intellectual ingenuity and capital, cultural bonds, and alliances, public schools became an autonomous and productive structure for African Americans.

Even more so, African Americans graduated from these schools with the ability to perform reading, writing, and arithmetic. Retention rates were high and protected from ethnic attachments and affiliations produced from these institutions. More importantly, a radical type of allegiance for the educational hearts and minds took hold of everyone, from faculty to parents to students who saw the value of productive schooling. Teachers and administrators lived in the community and sent their children to these schools. The community relied on each other to discipline, manage, and support the children. The best and brightest among them that were denied opportunities to compete in the mainstream economy worked as teachers or administrators. Students attending these schools received the very best the community had to offer. In many ways, the people made the public schools work for them despite external racial policies.

Shujaa (1996), in his book *Beyond Desegregation,* describes how African Americans were able to develop quality schools with minimal resources. Shujaa discusses how segregation during the Jim Crow Era forced African Americans to rely upon their own talents and skills to develop necessary institutions such as schools, organizations, churches, stores, and medical facilities. The black colleges and universities played an essential role by supplying trained individuals or intellectuals back to the community to promote sustainable, productive neighborhoods. Many of the teachers and administrators who taught in the schools were viewed as mentors and role models that could well equip and educate young people. Only in the rural parts of the south, where sharecropping was still very much a part of the African American economy, did you find teachers not as well trained.

Limited schooling and opportunities for African American educators in the south resulted in a less-trained workforce. In addition, the organization of the community, along with the clergy, helped establish quite a few public schools that were a quasi-functional component of the church. Although these schools were not ideal in nature, they shouldered the responsibility of teaching youth to prepare them to acquire opportunities in society. A large amount of future lawyers, physicians, and teachers came from the bowels of such institutions. Regardless of African Americans' status from racial practices, limited funding, or poor school structures, they viewed education as an external pathway to success. As a result, the community supported the efforts of public schooling because they believed it increased their opportunity to sustain, protect, and defend the progress of its people.

When the *Brown v. Board* (1954) decision was rendered, which legally desegregated schools allowing African Americans to enter schools where whites attended, it radically shifted school policymaking while reframing the way educators taught within traditional school settings. Although de jure segregation (which is enforced by law, as opposed to de facto segregation, which can occur when widespread individual preferences demand it) was not viewed as a complex problem for many southerners, the nation became aware of how damaging the policy was toward the African American community.

In some sectors, African American children believed white Americans were far superior or more intellectually capable than their cultural group (Kozol 2006). It appeared that whites had everything meaningful while African Americans barely subsisted. The result of this was psychologically damaging and caused the Supreme Court to rule in Brown v. the Board (1954) to favor the integration of African American children into white public schools so they could receive a better quality education. What the ruling got wrong was the idea that many African Americans were not receiving a quality education. As mentioned earlier, despite the limited resources and building structures that African Americans encountered, they were able to succeed in these segregated environments. Segregation forced African Americans to develop their own educational autonomy, which taught them how to economically provide for themselves. The result was profound because African Americans did not rely on white America to support education that they deemed important to sustain their community's existence. African Americans' economic and political gains were proof they saw themselves as important people despite having a second-class status.

The one thing most segregated public school environments fostered was cultural capitalism, the notion that a person's identity, heritage, and abilities must support his or her own community. Many segregated public school arrangements taught the importance of African Americans relying on their own to succeed in America. To do so required an education or skill to help empower the community. With the introduction of the new legislative policy that saw integration as necessary to spur a quality, fair education in the nation, the dynamics of cultural capitalism that once consumed the conscious souls of the African American community diminished.

The passage of *Brown v. Board* did two things: first, it stated that segregated schools were poor performing; second, it believed the schools were ill equipped to prepare African American children (Kozol 2012). It is interesting today that both arguments remain with us when dealing with the contemporary plight of African Americans attending public schools. Many of today's urban public schools are struggling to effectively prepare their students for the American economy. Yet there also remains a burgeoning African American middle class in America that successfully graduated from public schools and transitioned into the economy.

The *Brown v Board* ruling was clearly able to advance a segment of this community into greater opportunities they once were denied. The use of parental support, cultural norms and values, and financial resources helped progress a number of African Americans successful school navigations. Nonetheless, those African American youth who lacked the aforementioned protectorates attending public schools grew a distorted view of education and the positive impact it has on a community, coupled with the fact that not enough gifted African Americans returned to these communities to offer resources to advance young people. This has surely led to a crisis in public education for African Americans, which has fallen back on the teachers to correct. With limited tools, resources, and cultural bridges at their disposal, teachers and principals are fighting every day to find effective ways to improve the academic achievement of their learners.

In many circles today, people believe public education has failed the African American or minority communities. Despite the historical success in other communities, public education is struggling to survive in urban America. Communities that once were strong prior to integration now lack the economic infrastructure to sustain themselves. Also, the resources such as the people, institutions, and reformers that helped shape the institution of public education no longer exist. Instead, what has taken their place are business-minded, savvy people who see an opportunity to change the plight of African American learners. Whether good or bad, similar to the *Brown v. Board* decision, people are looking to improve urban schooling in America. The only questions are: Was there really something wrong with what worked before? Why did it work for groups of people who experienced radical repression and limited mainstream opportunities?

When Failure Became an Option:
The Plight of African American Learners in Urban Education

————

The history of African Americans in public education continues as an arduous journey. From de facto segregated, underfunded schools that were sadly brought forth by the *Brown v. Board* decision to decreasing graduation rates from high schools and colleges, an epidemic has surfaced, causing many people to argue what went wrong. Once upon a time, African Americans progressed through their own educational institutions and support networks to meet at least the minimum academic basics. Traditionally in many of these communities, excuses were rarely made to justify poor performance, despite the obstacles of racism. Regardless of the following effects: Jim Crow, disenfranchisement, broken legislative promises, terrorism, and the criminal justice system, African Americans were still able to rise above these challenges to move forward in the nation. The legacy of their survival has been a magnificent history of overcoming and a living testimony that declares, "When there is no way, God will make a way for a people to arise!"

More than ever today, too many African American youth are not connected to this powerful source of history. Many of them have unfortunately given up and accepted the negative notion that failure is an option. When urban students refused to live up to their ancestral legacy, which paved the way for them to exist, they embraced failure rather than success. What led to the plight of African Americans in education, where the dropout rate in many urban public schools across the nation is at 50 percent, to cause their acceptance of failure (Kozol 2012)? How do we help many of our young people escape this terrible notion that failure is an acceptable outcome?

The combination of the following factors has helped cause many African American youth to accept their plight: mass media, poor parenting skills, fatherless homes, economic inequities, institutional racism, and normalization of ghetto culture. Without question, these variables are affecting many American households curtailing youth pathway to excellence. Yet the rejection of the traditional value system that taught hard work, diligence, family responsibility, moral accountability, and respect are absolutely "tearing the soul" of America's cultural past. However, despite similar problematic issues, other cultural groups are not experiencing a 50 percent dropout rate from the nation's high schools (Jackson 2010). It's true these communities house many economic resources and social support systems that deter their youth from embracing failure or disproportional dropout rates; although money helps, it does not resolve their mediation and curtailment of these dilemmas.

Historically speaking, African Americans have traditionally paved the way for other minority groups to achieve an improved status in the nation (e.g., through Civil Rights legislation, affirmative action, and minority labor unions). African Americans have created a powerful blueprint for other minority groups to pattern after to help them ascend the social and educational ladders. The failure to apply this same blueprint to the educational dilemma of African American youth proves that the cultural bridges and capital that once defined the community are absent.

With the absence of much-needed cultural protectorates, a gulf has emerged between those African Americans who connect with their historical legacy and those who simply do not embrace their roots. The segment of African Americans who are guided by traditional concepts, beliefs, and parental support mechanisms continue to assert themselves quite well in public schools; on the contrary, far too many negative behaviors in schools have surfaced from students who lack cultural guidance and direction to understand the value of education. From wearing sagging pants, to possessing "bad" attitudes toward learning, to unethical dress code violations, anti-intellectual mentalities, and a high disrespect toward educators or supervisors, a new generation of African Americans has arrived.

Although these students compose a minority of the population in some schools, in some educational environments they have completely taken over. Intuitively speaking, when directing our attention to this specific set of learners, stereotypical notions and perceptions of African American inferiority surfaces, bringing forth either consigned or counseled means to deal with this crisis. Let's be clear: majority of African Americans and other cultural groups understand the value of correcting this ordeal. To move forward as a nation, all groups must become involved and not excluded to effectively progress.

To help correct this issue, it is dire that educational agencies such as think tanks become involved right away to steer these learners toward a new direction. No longer can African Americans continue to only expect external community agencies to provide for their youth. Strategic methods must also come from internal forces within neighborhood arrangements since these communities know what they need to improve their educational status. As a result, it's important that independent social institutions emerge from these disadvantaged communities to help develop, train, and prepare youth leaders to counter this challenge. Actions such as these will help spur meaningful transformation in urban education.

Groups like the Black Star Project, headed by Phillip Jackson, are already working diligently to remedy this crisis. The Black Star Project is a think-tank and educational support system designed to strengthen African Americans experience and learning outcomes in education. They offer Saturday academies and mentor activities to nurture, enrich, and support students' school outcomes. This educational support alone, although helpful, will not entirely rectify the problem. To close the ever-widening achievement gap, similar to past struggles, African Americans must greatly rely on themselves by empowering their youth. To successfully break the vicious pattern of educational failure, the emergence and collective support of external agencies, African American leadership, educators, and intellectuals must serve the community to bring about a new sense of progress in urban education.

Transitions

My final year at the alternative high school, September 2000 to June 2001, was filled with unexpected anxiety regarding what may happen to our school, along with trying to grow as a teacher. This year also brought a new sense of urgency and preparation because I knew I required more support to help me develop. Additionally, I had just completed my master's degree in education, so I was seeking a new opportunity elsewhere. My first child had arrived, so coupled with my wife attending school and not working, I needed to make a little more money. I soon took a part-time job on the weekend at a railroad company as a custodial worker while applying to several non-alternative traditional schools. At the time I felt I could actually learn more working in a traditional learning environment while acquiring additional supportive resources. Also, I believed the school enrollment would improve to make my employment situation more stable. The downside of my moving on would affect my classroom autonomy; the creative freedom of developing my own curriculum would be curtailed to testing, and I would lose valuable colleagues and a supportive principal who looked after my needs as a professional. Change was good, but at what cost?

With the school being evaluated by the district, I became more concerned about my job status rather than the collegial environment where I worked. It affected me to learn that our budget was to become further reduced, which meant even fewer resources for the classroom. I got sick of using old, outdated books. Our enrollment issues were probably due to the district's development of high school support services (e.g., freshmen academies, summer transition programs, credit retrieval opportunities), systems that I felt should have always been adopted to help keep students in school.

As an educator, I was glad to see the development of such programs that could advance students through high school. However, there were still learners who could not succeed in a traditional model, which required an alternative learning environment. I knew the district would always need alternative arrangements to support their retention rates. It also appeared that our students' academic testing levels in reading and math lowered from previous years. Too many students were just giving up on school and no longer cared about learning. I was spending more and more time trying to convince students why they should learn the information. Despite my ability to create stimulating and engaging lessons, a number of students struggled to maintain their grades in other classes. This was when I felt it necessary to develop a mentor program to help some of our students maintain their focus in school.

The mentor program I developed was borrowed from an organization called, Hundred Black Men. The objective of the program was to provide resources, external support systems, and role models to help guide young black men through education. Although there was a great need for a female program, which existed in various parts of the city, I took the initiative to make use of the male mentor component because our school's population was mostly black males. My revision of certain aspects of the Hundred Black Men to match it with important characteristics of our school helped to establish the mentor program. The program's name was Rites of Direction. The program occurred after school, two days a week for two hours.

I crafted notions that focused on

(1) improving retention and attendance rates;

(2) assigning role models to support students' progression; and

(3) advancing males' entry into higher educational programs.

On a monthly basis, I invited a special guest speaker to talk to and encourage our kids. I had students investigate summer internship or employment opportunities to increase their school interest. I wished I had connections with professionals who worked in a medical, technical, or service-orientated field. Although the Hundred Black Men did help to provide mentors and various contacts, it was difficult trying to connect students to summer internship or employment opportunities they desired to pursue upon graduation because a lot of employment firms or agencies had limited funded and strict deadlines that students were unable to satisfy. The program also offered students role-play scenarios or real-life problem situations to solve. Like so many of our urban male student population, too many of them did not know how to seek alternative choices to avoid a conflict or solve a problem. Instead, they acted out raw emotions to handle their problems, making the situation worst. Some of my males already had arrest records before they turned eighteen years of age. Without proper tutelage and guidance, I did not feel they could make proper choices to succeed.

What I found most interesting about my experience working in urban schools is that like me, there are a lot of educators working before or after school to help students. These are the dedicated professionals who some people do not acknowledge. The teachers at my school never received payment for volunteering their time and energy to improve students because they saw a need to help support students' progress in school. One of the educators at my school created a sewing class to help teach young ladies how to create their own clothes. Another instructor held a chess club to teach students how to think and problem solve. Someone else decided to have a beginner's swimming class, where they used their own money to rent a park district's swimming pool for a couple of hours every two weeks. Examples such as these are replete with the various ways educators work diligently to help support students.

As a result of our school being an alternative high school, existing on a skeletal budget with low enrollment, after-school programs were not funded. To do anything required the volunteer efforts of teachers to fill the void. This is even more common today, where far too many schools do not have the money to offer after-school programs. Most notably, some schools have had to cut their sports programs and other extracurricular activities to not terminate teachers or support staff.

I learned quickly that volunteering after school, raising a small family, and working part time for eight hours on the weekend was exhausting. I knew in my soul I could not keep this up. In fact, my efforts at home were diminishing and detracted from the quality time I was giving my own child. Quite simply, I needed a new opportunity to make a little more money. I had heard that some schools provided teachers with stipends to manage after-school programs. This would allow me to quit my custodial job on the weekend. Also, I learned that a number of schools offered professional mentors for educators to help them grow. Although I had recently completed my master's degree, I believed I required more collegial support in my particular subject area to help me increase student achievement.

My principal was terrific providing me with strategies I could use in the classroom. The only problem was she was not a history teacher, and I needed to have someone help me sort out the content covered in this subject to advance students' academic skills. Teaching critical reading and writing were the primary goals of my curriculum, yet I believed there were more strategic or effective ways this could be utilized to support students' growth. Since my principal really did not have the funding to send me to professional workshops, I had to find ways to come up with the money myself so I could attend.

What I found interesting about attending some of the workshops was that although it was helpful identifying classroom strategies, there was just too much content to process at one time. It was clear to me, like my first year of teaching, that it was important to apply one concept at a time in the classroom. Similar to everything else, it would take time before I could master the strategy's intent on students. Moreover, educators are provided a great deal of strategies to apply in the classroom to solve their instructional challenges or dilemmas. Some administrators expect teachers to learn how to apply them immediately to increase student performance or output, yet when they don't, they are viewed as incompetent or ineffective. I also felt it was important to test the effectiveness of theoretical strategy on our learners before we declared it noteworthy. As the case with many of the strategies at educational conferences, some "expert" researched how well the strategy worked with a distinct population of learners. However, just because the results were effective with one set of learners does not mean it applies to every student. Quite a few of the strategies at the conferences I attended applied to teaching middle-class student populations, not disadvantaged inner-city youth. As a result, I constantly found myself revising or tweaking the strategy to apply to my learners. I appreciated the knowledge, information, and expertise acquired at the forums; I only wished the discussions were yielded from teachers who had experienced my own population of learners. Over time I was able to learn from educators with similar experiences in the trenches and apply their strategies to my learners. The presenters that related to my experiences helped me grow professionally in education.

Despite my best efforts and sincere time and energy at the school, I knew it was time for me to move on. I received an interview over the summer at the end of my third year of teaching. The school was situated in Englewood, a poor-to-middle income neighborhood located in the heart of the city. Like so many other urban neighborhoods in Chicago, a skeletal economic infrastructure tried to sustain and support the community. Abandoned buildings, broken glass, with young men standing on the corner defined some aspects of the community; on the other hand, the neighborhood harbored nice homes, small businesses, and a determined working-class population. Aspects of the school defined both realities: young people who came from broken, dysfunctional homes with a negative attitude toward schooling versus students nurtured in a supportive family structure that valued education. I believed it would be interesting to work in such an environment where I could reach out to those students with some set of challenges while attending to the needs of traditional learners who desired an educational opportunity.

I answered questions during the interview that primarily focused on my ability to motivate, engage, and improve the academic skills of learners. I cited the numerous examples of how I planned to affect the students' academic growth and development at the school while describing some of my past achievements working with a similar population of learners. I also discussed my usage of the mentor program, which I felt impressed the interviewing committee. They were highly interested to learn more about the effectiveness of the program and whether I would attempt to apply it to their school if hired. I ensured them that I would love to develop the same type of program at their school to work with challenged learners.

My questions for the interview committee revolved around teacher-mentor programs, supportive resources, and the academic status of the school, questions I did not ask when I started my first school job. The answers that I received helped me ascertain that the school was committed to cultivating and supporting effective teachers who could enhance their school. There were challenges, but issues that could be resolved with a committed learning community of educators. In the end, this is what attracted me more to the school than ever before. Not to mention I believed I would enjoy the next educational challenges that lay ahead.

When I heard I'd gotten the new teaching job, I was elated. On top of the new teaching and learning opportunities the job offered, I would make about $12,000 more in pay, belong to a teachers union, and receive more available teacher resources. Now, I had to separate from my former school. Besides writing a letter of resignation, I decided to visit with my principal to express my sincere thanks and support of me working at the school. We had a very engaging forty-five-minute conversation on the state of education, my new job, and why I decided to leave. Our discussion was well intended and particularly focused on my transition.

As I told her, I believed the status of the school was "up in the air," so I felt I required more instructional support and required another challenge. My principal for three years was always supportive of my teaching style, strategy, and connection to my students. As she put, "If the kids seem to enjoy and act excited about what they were learning, teaching is taking place." She also saw my efforts working with the students and appreciated my dedication to the school.

I continue to use my former principal as a reference and mentor to help guide me through education. Today, the school barely exists on a skeletal budget. Two years after I left, the school was moved to a smaller location. Several teachers were laid off. Eventually, my principal retired and today serves as a mentor for principals in the school system.

Other collegial members from our community adjusted to the changes and moved forward in the profession. A former colleague is a successful principal at a high school; several others work in a non-alternative environments like I do; and two others are now junior college professors. Although change did eventually force our faculty to transition into new opportunities, we all took valuable lessons from our school experience, which included community, congeniality, collegiality, and the culture of teaching and learning.

Before starting my new job, I acquired my schedule to review the classes I was teaching. This time around I was teaching freshmen, so I really couldn't interview former teachers. Although I did investigate the students' feeder schools or partnering schools and analyzed their eighth-grade reading scores, I really didn't know a lot about the learners entering my class. During this time I received entry into Roosevelt's doctoral program to study education administration and curriculum development. I had always wanted to lead a school while working with teachers to support and develop the necessary changes to improve education. I understood this would be a great deal of work along with learning a new job. Again, I strongly believed my family suffered with my ambition and desire to professionally grow and improve. I further believed that entry into this program would equip me with even more strategies to apply in my classroom to support the teachers at my school.

Long before the day ends, a teacher's work is never done. Quality teaching involves a type of dedication and commitment that surely impacts an educator's personal life for years to come. Not to mention, quite a few teachers continue their education while working during the school year. Upon my starting my graduate courses, I found myself immersed in the literature and information that shapes the foundation of quality teaching and learning. From reading Piaget, Dewey, Tyler, Wiggins, Sergiovanni, and numerous other scholars, my perspectives of education radically shifted.

However, what I found troubling was that the school system, as quite often the case, scarcely adapted or applied existing scholarly works into education. Although my district used the magical phrase "children first," there was often limited support to ensure educators, principals, and students succeeded in the school. It took the initiative of teachers and administrators to study, investigate, and research the various ways to improve how students learn. Besides offering workshops that again did not often resonate with urban populations, the system threatened, imposed, and abrasively informed the professional community of what to do.

I further begin discovering that the quality of teaching and learning was not a series of strategies, as I once thought, but rather first rooted in effective instruction. When teachers understand themselves and their students' learning styles, special needs, readiness, and reading differences, a teacher can become effective. This also meant that teachers could teach with a purpose when they know their content, students, and the subject's objective. This is where I believed I needed to grow professionally: how to master the content well enough so that the students would really be engaged, which would improve their academic skills. Here I discovered the importance of teaching skills over content. For teaching history, this would become a difficult challenge because so much content exists in the subject. The great thing about working at my new job was that I belonged to a department; unfortunately, I was the only one teaching history at my last school, which brought a great amount of pressure. I felt that if I could share and learn from other history teachers in the department, it would further prepare me to learn more about my subject's intent and objective.

Change is necessary to continue to grow as an instructor, whether good or bad, and a transition helps an educator develop. This is what I learned during my fourth year of teaching. So much work went into my fourth year to become an effective educator that today I still don't know how I survived the school year. Teaching freshmen learners was a new challenge because a lot of the students had to be taught "how to do school," which meant instructing them on organization, code of conduct, planning, and studying. Our school lacked a classroom advisory, which I felt would have helped teach students these powerful traits. Eventually, in the following year, our school provided an advisory class, and it took some time to learn how to effectively plan and apply it to meet the needs of our students. Nevertheless, it helped us to learn our students better while teaching important social and academic skills.

What I found most interesting transitioning into my new school was meeting my colleagues. I could tell the ones who were still very enthusiastic and excited about teaching versus the ones who had simply been in the system too long. With the exception of a few teachers, most of us had instructional goals we wanted to prepare students to help them achieve a successful school year. The few teachers that seem to struggle were "burned out" by the system; therefore, they did not harbor any good expectations for the school. Educators such as these have become disappointed from the useless bureaucracy, methods, and practices of the school system, which causes them to have a pragmatic attitude toward teaching. I always felt that if I ever acquired such a trait, it would be time for me to leave teaching. Although at times I found myself disappointed with the way things were handled by administrators and the district office, I could not afford to let it affect my attitude toward students or the teaching and learning practice.

At the beginning of the school year I made it a point to introduce myself to the custodial staff, security team, and secretaries and converse with them. I learned from my previous school that becoming friends with them made a teacher's job less complicated, from thoroughly cleaning your classroom before an unannounced administrative inspection to keeping you informed about all the latest school news helped manage your day. Befriending these professionals allow an educator to become more of a supportive member of the community. I found that custodians, secretaries, and security guards are leaders and educators. They serve as powerful members of a school community because they talk, mentor, and help students make good decisions. In addition, a lot of this staff lives in the community and know the families of the students. I often sought information about a student (e.g., living arrangements, addresses, phone numbers, etc.) when the school or district lacked the information.

Far too many schools do not value this population of professionals or make skillful use of them. They can dutifully assist educators by supplying important school information, mentoring, and offering support to special programs. In many ways these professionals are the social workers of a school community. They check in with students, talk to them about the "realness" of their day, make recommendations for their learning and living situations, and offer assistance and support to extended educational programs. These professionals are truly the eyes and ears of a school community.

So here I began a new school and professional responsibility. I promised myself to work smarter and more efficiently this time around to continue as an effective instructor. Although I was new to the building, I believed I had made the necessary plans to become acquainted with the teachers. I had even volunteered two days a week, for a couple of hours, working summer school to assist a freshmen world studies teacher. This provided me with the necessary leverage to meet students and members of the school community. I visited two feeder schools to learn more about the type of students that would enter my classroom. Although I did not get a chance to interview the teachers, talking with the principal and a few faculty members helped me plan my instruction during the first five weeks of school. Conversing and acquainting myself with members of the support staff furthered my successful transition into the new school. In the end, I felt prepared to begin my new school while taking graduate school classes. I was excited about the upcoming year and expected a successful transition.

Personal Saga

When all was said and done, I expended a minimum amount of energy at home and sacrificed my personal time for the school. When I looked up my daughter was four, a second child was on her way, my father had passed, and my mom was ill from breast cancer. Life was seemingly passing me by, and I wondered, *Is this field of education worth all the personal sacrifices?* My journey, yet incomplete, invested a tremendous of time and energy to a profession that did not provide a great deal of revenue or return on my professional investment. Yet the satisfaction lay in the amount of energy, time, and sacrifice I had placed into young adults. I could see the fruits of my labor by witnessing their entry into college, newfound professional interests, positive behavioral changes, and a new respect for themselves. All of this took time, of course, as people matured, aged, or grew up. But it was the quality time invested in young people that no money, test scores, or budget could ever measure. This was truly the sacrifice and pleasure of teaching, and it was my personal saga.

Before my father passed, I had taken a month from school to help nurse him. During his final days he told me all the wonderful things he attempted to pass on to me while growing up. I understood completely what my "pops" was communicating to me because for years he had served as my teacher. He taught me how to value life, education, sports, and religion. More importantly, he taught me how to become a man. Today, I dedicate a great deal of his teaching to other young men in education I encounter. In fact, I try to epitomize the values he shared with me toward my students. There is a certain tone and appeal I reflect toward my students, similar to a father figure, when trying to guide, correct, and mentor them.

I also quote my old man a lot when transferring knowledge or wisdom to the male students in my classroom or mentor program. The development of a mentor program was rooted in my experience of having a positive male role model. After all, I knew the importance of having a father in the home and how it impacted my life growing up. Today, I witness a great deal of young men who have benefited from having positive male figures. Some are fathers, electricians, musicians, engineers, sanitation workers, or policemen. A number of them have gone on to college, some finishing and others not; however, the bottom line is that they turned out okay.

Many males in our schools today lack role models and are in desperate need of positive male teachers. African American males, especially, require more quality mentors and role models because far too many of their fathers are absent. As a result, they struggle in school and harbor a lot of resentment and anger toward other males. This is why I have always found a need to dedicate and commit myself to my father's legacy when teaching young African American males. Although education does lack African American male teachers, female educators are just as important in their lives. Educators are constantly filling a void for young people, families, and communities they serve. Without teachers, many communities would really suffer from the lack of human services educators provide.

My greatest maternal figures, besides my own mom, during my professional and student life during this time were my principal and doctoral chair. These women helped provide me with great insight and perspective toward education. They identified solutions, they helped identify research to support my graduate writing, and they pushed me to succeed.

My mother also did this while encouraging me to push on when I felt like I wanted to quit school while working. She would always whisper, "You will do it."

Without their positive demands, I would not have completed school and grown as an educator. In a way, this is what teachers constantly do with their students. They demand the very best from them when students want to quit. Teachers coach their students to succeed despite the challenges they encounter. Moreover, they believe in the students. All of these attributes I applied in the classroom to coach, mentor, and teach young people. I gave them advice, I helped them write papers, and I counseled them through their trials. I gave up a lot of time to ensure their success.

Again, this is what teachers do to make sure students are learning. So now when I hear how teachers are accused of failing students, I wonder what a lot young people would do without educators. Maybe society and communities have failed young people, not teachers? How about their failure is due, in large part, to our fault as a nation for not providing enough resources and support to help young people reach their potential? Besides blaming educators, maybe we need to take a good look at what we really value in this country.

We need to continue to teach and instill values into our young people that they can always treasure and apply. Such values are what allowed me to attend graduate school and not give up on my desires to improve as an educator. Despite school taking away the remaining personal time I could spare with my love ones, it helped me grow into a better person. These were the wonderful concepts and values my mom had transferred to me. When my mother became really sick, I knew my time with her was near an end. I had to take off from work to nurse her while working on my dissertation. It took a considerable amount of spiritual energy and personal wherewithal to help her during her final days.

Like my father before, she showered me with the appeal to keep working hard while taking care of my family. Her love, for many years, provided me with a resolve to continue to aspire professionally. So when she passed, I always felt I lost my dearest friend and best supporter. Her powerful life lessons are concepts that I strive to pass on to my children and students. For years as an educator, I have always tried to provide students with an appeal to appreciate their life journey while loving the people that exist within their circle. Education requires a teacher to make a special kind of connection with students to help them mature and develop. A successful educator cannot just teach from a test or curriculum to guide students. Rather, it is important that their focus relies on the ability to make a personalized connection with students. I refer to this as a customized education.

Similar to visiting a store, business owners have to demonstrate personalized connections with their cliental to continue to attract revenue. The customer service and relationship has to be of quality, the product has to connect with and appeal to the buyer, and the environment must welcome the consumer.

This same logic applies in education. The teachers have to connect their lessons to the student, which can be accomplished by building a connection with the student (e.g., knowing their interests, goals, and personal narratives). The product deals with the way a teacher instructs or sells their lesson to the students to convince them as to why they should learn it. Some argue that the teacher in this fashion is like a salesman. The teacher has to sell the lesson, like a product, to convince students as to why they need the knowledge.

An environment deals with the culture and climate of the classroom. A teacher's classroom atmosphere has to make students feel safe, secure, and comfortable enough to want to learn. As an educator, it is important to nurture and establish these important concepts to students. In many ways, it is similar to being a mother that makes every attempt to make the student loved, supported, and cherished to progress their learning. In an odd sort of way, a mother is always selling something warm, sweet, and good to convince her children to efficiently produce.

As my mother convinced me to excel and strive for the best, I work hard to apply this principle while teaching students. Like most educators, they have to make the lesson come to life to convince students why they should learn it. Testing and grades do not always satisfy the educational aspiration of students, although they help, but the way the lesson is packaged and constructed convinces students why they should value the subject's information. It is the love of learning, the joy of discovery, the appeal for information and knowledge that a teacher strives to reach with his or her students. To do so requires nurturing, dedication, and the possession of maternal instincts to soothe, correct, and guide young people to academic success.

As my career continues in this wonderful field, I have gained and lost a lot. The personal sacrifice of a teacher beckons them to grow, learn, and experience challenges in the profession. Teaching offers powerful life lessons that can be passed down and applied to students. Since our experiences and past endeavors define us as educators, there are a lot of important principles we need to transfer to our students. Life lessons will help them grow and develop; they can learn how to treasure information and knowledge. When teachers teach, they pass on powerful personal traits, knowingly or unknowingly, to their students. When teachers teach, they learn from others and grow to understand the meaning of their profession. When teachers teach, they exist on a personal journey that grows into a saga of its own.

The Personal Side of Teaching

Quite a few teachers quit the profession after their six years of teaching, some sooner due to the demands and constraints of the field (Wong 2009). What teachers new to the profession soon discover is that personal experiences inside and outside the classroom effects how they connect with and teach students. Extraneous or external variables present dilemmas to any professional, especially for people that have to work in a human service capacity. Administrators or managers often refer to the term professionalism when describing the expectations, norms, and obligations a worker exhibits in his or her occupation. Personal ordeals or challenges can truly impact an educator's ability to relate to students. Educators especially have to be humane and serve as a sort of protective guardian when working with troubled or challenged learners. That is why, when educators are able to connect with students, it reflects a true love of teaching and learning. It's not uncommon to hear educators entering the profession state the main reason being their love of working with children. They treasure the personal and human side of the field. When an educator can make a personal connection to students and value the interpersonal relationships developed in the classroom, it makes for a fine educator and classroom atmosphere.

In many ways, a teacher's "true" persona emerges in a classroom. When a teacher truly cares about his or her profession and demonstrates a dedicated love toward students, a personalized instruction emerges in the classroom. Personalized instruction allows a teacher to really know their students or feel the pulse of their classroom to effectively engage them. In many urban settings, a teacher has to be able to deliver this type of instruction to academically prepare students. Without doing so, a subject's information or knowledge often cannot be ascertained by students. As a result of so many students manifesting emotional and psychological scars from their family and community environments, it becomes extremely important for an educator to know the emotional profile of the students.

Quite a few educators discuss the challenges working in urban environments, where students come from disadvantaged settings. It is not uncommon to have children walk into a teacher's class early in the morning, "mean mugging" or displaying a face of frustration toward them with an attitude. When a relationship is established with that child, a teacher understands right away that something is wrong. This is when intervention skills go into effect, where the teacher works his or her interpersonal magic to resolve the issue enough to prepare the student to focus on today's instruction. Although the problem will require continued attention and support, for now the teacher has to get the student ready to learn.

On the other side of the coin is a teacher with poor relationships with students or maybe simply having a bad day. This usually results in disaster with the student's problem growing worse, leading to behavioral issues in the classroom. In such classroom arrangements you find students with their heads down on their desks, zoned out from instruction. Teachers who do not effectively know how to deal with students who express their personal, emotional issues in their classroom have a difficult time staying in the profession. Again, so much goes into effective teaching that the academic side of education is just one component that makes up the profession.

Teaching specifically includes

preparation,

research,

mastery of content,

interpersonal skills,

counseling,

discipline, and

management (Wong 2009).

There are other aspects missed in this analysis, but the main thing that stands out is that successful teaching requires the application of multiple strategies to meet the needs of learners.

Another important factor that deals with the personal side of instruction is the ability of the instructor to make the curriculum come to life. When an instructor understands the pupils in front of them, they know their likes and dislikes. In today's world, an assignment has to be made interesting for a student to internalize the goal of the instruction. With modern media outlets and tools such as iPods, video gaming systems, cable TV, and other technological devices, this generation of Americans are easily distracted.

Neil Postman (2005) refers to this as "amusing ourselves to death" when detailing the harmful effects of technology. From his assertion, technology has helped lower young people's attention spans and intellectual applications. For teachers to be successful in a classroom, they cannot simply focus on teaching to a test or direct instructional strategies. Rather, they must be innovative clinicians when connecting the subject to the learner. An effective teacher can take any piece of information and make it become interesting and engaging to the students.

What allows the teacher to do so is reflected in his or her ability to relate and connect the content to learners. Having a strong personal attachment to students allows the teacher to know what students will find interesting, engaging, and informative versus boring, dry, and ineffective. This is when not only good research comes to play with teachers investigating quality lessons for students but also their ability to differentiate or diversify the information to match specific learning styles. Of course, this takes time and patience to acquire this trait, which quite often does not occur in a six-year time frame. Differentiation alone cannot be achieved in a workshop to apply to learners. Like anything else, a teacher needs to apply the strategies before determining their effectiveness. Teachers who struggle to build personalized connections with their students struggle with developing engaging lessons. In some instances, they may even give up on discovering what works for their learners and begin to focus on the bottom line. This is where the frailty and danger of the testing has affected teaching. Too many schools have made teachers become overly concerned about test scores to keep their jobs. Therefore, it is not surprising educators tailor lessons toward exams rather than focus on the personal side of teaching. In fact, they may even find it foolish that time and effort needs to be spent on getting to know a student. When testing overtakes the curriculum and determines the effectiveness of an educator, personalizing the curriculum become secondary.

To build an effective and engaging classroom, educators have to exhibit their personal side of teaching. This not only includes knowing your students but also understanding how to best engage them. Despite the personal challenges students may be experiencing, it is essential an educator reaches them to help them achieve their potential. In some ways, personal challenges should be used as powerful teaching moments to prepare and engage students. Whether coming from a teacher or student, the life lessons learned are effective strategies to teach students how to overcome and persevere beyond challenges. Effective teaching should not deal with just academics but also with the interpersonal side of instruction. When students understand how the subject relates to them, they radically understand the meaning and purpose of the lesson's objective. More importantly, they build connections with the material. When this happens, students learn the value and practicality of a lesson. "Real" teaching can only exist if a personal side of instruction manifests itself in the lesson. This allows specific students to escape the chaotic realities they are forced to survive; it furthers their investment of information similar to listening to an iPod; and effective instruction teaches them how to apply information. When the personal side of education manifests itself in the classroom, students love learning and value schooling.

PART III

It's the Journey

How a Culturally Relevant Model Adds Educational Value

––––––

The value of a culturally relevant education relies on how one responds to the question, "Is it the journey or the destination?" Both schools of thought are important. Say you're planning a trip. If someone or something is waiting on you, then you only desire the destination. Your focus will be on getting there as directly and efficiently as possible. Under these circumstances, the distance alone may seem so far away as to be unattainable in a satisfactory amount of time, so you may be willing to take as many shortcuts as possible to help get you to where you're going as fast as possible. Any deviation from the planned route would be considered an inconvenience, maybe even an annoyance.

However, if you value the journey, the distance no longer becomes an obstacle no matter how far away you must travel. The focus, instead, is on how meaningful each passing milestone becomes. Landmarks such as the Statue of Liberty, the Grand Canyon, or the Taj Mahal will enrich the journey, not distract from the destination. Even setbacks such as lost luggage or a misread map will allow for a "teachable" moment on how to regroup or handle a crisis.

Many scholars throughout time, including in Ancient Greece, believed in the journey rather than the destination in regard to an educated life. It was Socrates who stated, "An unexamined life is not worth living." The Greeks created a theory on education called "*paideia.*" Oversimplified, paideia is the use of the mind and body working in conjunction to achieve an appreciation for learning that relies heavily on cultural development. This development of the mind does not end merely because the student receives the equivalent of a diploma and therefore no longer needs school. In fact, the students of this school of thought are actually motivated to indefinitely continue learning. Learning becomes something they take pride in for their own self-worth, their community, and their culture.

In direct contrast to the Ancient Greeks, in many of America's public schools, especially those in urban settings, destination graduation is the only option given to students. This means students are taught to focus on credits, grades, and test scores to reflect how much they have mastered or learned. Hence, the only thing that matters are standardized test performance. Many of these schools will teach to the test and then test and retest students up to five times a year to gauge their progress. The students' actual grades, grade-point averages, and whether they are able to effectively read and write or perform on a college or professional level—where standardized test are no longer even relevant—are often overlooked. Basing student success solely on the successful completion of the twelfth grade or even how well they performed on a test, despite whether they have truly learned and retained anything, is one of the leading factors as to why these schools have such a high rate of students who give up on their education and drop out of school.

While it is far too easy for curriculum creators to blame outside factors impacting student performance, the fact remains that the dropout rate is so high that social factors alone can no longer be solely to blame for student progress. If 1 percent of students were failing, that may be because of the student and social indicators. If half the student population is failing, then there is an issue with the curriculum or pedagogy. As it stands in many of the largest school districts in the country, more than 60 percent of the students score below grade level—this is not merely an issue that needs to be addressed, it is a crisis-level epidemic (Ravitch 2010). How are schools addressing this epidemic? Many in these failing districts are being directed to shut out the voices of the students and parents and are becoming more stringent in their policies that police students' behavior, requiring that more and more students are labeled "special needs" than ever before. But any physician will tell you that you cannot treat the patient while at the same time ignoring the symptoms.

Having a cultural responsive pedagogy allows the educator to listen to students' needs, address those needs, and connects the educator with the students, the parents, and the community in a more impactful way. This model of teaching allows the educator to learn who the students are and relate the curriculum to the student. This model differs greatly from the current model in place, where the onus is on the student to relate to the material being taught, and somehow from this deficit, bridge the gap from what the student knows to what the teacher wants him or her to learn.

The deficit model in place now says to minority students that who they are and where they come from is somehow less valuable than what they should want for themselves, so they need to test well in order to have a better, more meaningful life. That is a judgment call the school system is making, and it comes from an extremely patronizing point of view. Demeaning someone's identity all the while simultaneously saying you love him or her and want to help is counterproductive. It is the educator saying that who you are now is not valuable, but who I will make you into will perhaps, someday, be someone of worth. It is not surprising that under this model students have yet to become motivated or engaged in their learning, perhaps because this deficit model is less about teaching and more about reprogramming these students' identities.

This blanket denial of student cultures and communities is negating their voices. Any sign of a student's frustration is silenced behind terms like "special needs" or "emotional immaturity." Instead of connecting students to a curriculum that can address their cultural needs and motivate them to learn for learning's sake with a supportive theme on overall graduation, students are being set up for a longer term and more debilitating failure—college and life. In the short term, in some cases at least 50 percent of minority students do not graduate from secondary school (Jackson 2010). But much worse than that statistic is that even those who do graduate and go on to college, many drop out of college (or are kicked out) due to poor academic performance and lack of preparedness.

By weighing destination graduation so heavily, students are getting out of high school only to still be left behind in college, graduate schools, and in life. This not only means students are ill prepared to compete on a national or global level, but by failing to be prepared for life after graduation, these students are recycled back into poverty or prisons, and their children are in the same failing educational system that failed their parents. Is that progress?

This practice cannot continue unchecked. The current educational curriculum must go beyond, "Yes, I will graduate," and even further than, "Yes, I will go to college." Data shows that getting into college does not mean that the educational battle is over for minority students and their socioeconomic issues have been resolved. The curriculum must have a more holistic approach to students' needs. It must employ strategies that are able to address more than the end result of graduation and empower students to embrace the educational process. A cultural relevant education model can address these needs by adding value to the overall and long-term impact of the educational process by offering students more options.

My Philosophy

Since graduating from Roosevelt University, I have learned the main difference between theoretical constructs and practical applications. In many ways my dissertation, research analysis, and critical perspectives about education have been tried and tested. For starters, upon graduating from my program I took an administrative position in a very challenging school district. The district, for the most part, had a terrible school climate and culture, which translated into inadequate student performance, high teacher and administrative turnover, and poor parental relationship and support. After two years of administrative work as a social science curriculum coach, I returned to my old stomping ground, only to discover the school was enduring a major transition under new school reform measures. This brought a certain amount of professional instability along with low teacher and student attrition rates. My next journey sent me to a newly modeled charter framework, a performing-arts high school. It is here that I begin to see my professional growth develop and expand while my knowledge of instructional best practices blossomed.

From working as an adjunct professor to a high school instructor and administrator has taught me valuable educational lessons. Essentially, my dissertation focused on cultural responsive education and how such an instructional pedagogy would increase student efficacy, engagement, and school performance. What I have discovered since my research is that far too many schools depend on standardized testing to frame their curriculum. As a result, schools were not entirely focused on curriculum development. Instead, they aligned their pedagogy to support college readiness standards. This caused many students to receive drill-kill prep exercises or direct teaching lessons that focus on taking a standardize test, which hurt any curriculum perspectives or content teachers believed would enhance students' intellectual and global competency. It was a basic formula schools applied: students should learn skills over content, meaning they should improve their skills through test-prep instructional focus versus curriculum content standards or enrichment.

This was a terrible approach from my analysis because it would further disengage "borderline" or low-performing learners from school, diminish the value of the curriculum, and deconstruct cultural history and literary studies. Henceforth, I became agitated working in contemporary education because I felt it underserved the needs and interests of the majority of the student populations that were English learning students, minorities, or special needs. To more effectively service such students that I believed were being written off, I returned to school to acquire a special-needs endorsement. I felt this would equip me to better advocate for students while trying to instructionally balance skill-based instruction with curriculum knowledge.

The majority of special-need learners require not only skill-based improvement but a greater knowledge-base understanding of curriculum content. Teaching students with these special qualities is both unique and enriching. I have learned so much working with this student population. First and foremost, I truly understand what is meant by the coined instructional term, "differentiation." Not only does this allow an instructor to design and add different layers to their learning practice, it enhances the teacher's ability to meet the learner where he or she is in skill development.

The most important lesson that I have learned is that *all* students have different learning styles and no one application or theory effectively resolves their needs. As a result, this spurred my perspectives on education to shift from a theoretical perspective to more of an applied methodology. Although educational research should encompass both, in some instances it has yet to achieve this symbiotic outcome.

My most recent investigative research endeavor has led me to want to write more about my educational experiences while also discussing how a cultural responsive curriculum is effective within an integrated, value-centered pedagogy. From my most recent publication and understanding, what enhances students' educational responses to acquire an enriched educational experience is rooted in their set of values. Values promote, dictate, and add meaning to students' cultural context that surround and shape their lives.

My years of interacting with learners from poor economic backgrounds and troubled school climates have taught me that value-based and cultural education, as a learning practicum and applied approach, are uniquely bonded. Ultimately, what helped shape this ideological shift were my enriched interactions and connections with students who struggled. They exhibited challenges with not only connecting or responding to the curriculum but incorporating the value processes of learning to motivate their interest and connection to school. Having the ability to work in a creative school that embraces diverse curriculum applications, models art-integrated pedagogy, and sustains a multicultural and liberal school environment allowed me to rediscover the benefits of applying a value-cultural relevant framework in education.

The Intent of Teaching

As mentioned in the previous chapter, education is similar to Greek philosophy. It is about the spiritual and mental journey of a person's discovery for truth, moral direction, and harmonic balance. As Christ once stated, "How a man thinks, so is he" (Proverbs 23:7). A great deal of liberal education centers on this philosophical notion, especially when dealing with how curriculums should be developed to enhance the "whole" human being. Liberal education is not simply just about literacy and numeracy; rather, it deals with the arts, music, culture, and religion. A complete human being is a whole person who appreciates the way the world interconnects, develops, and enhances human capital. A comprehensive liberal arts education allows people to discover a deeper appreciation for the universe that an omnipotent power built.

As an educator, it is important to help students realize the importance of the journey versus the destination. The development of the mind and spirit does not end merely because the student receives the equivalent of a diploma and therefore no longer needs school. Students that receive a meaningful, well-rounded liberal arts education are actually motivated to continue learning indefinitely. Learning becomes something they take pride in for their own self-worth, their community, and their culture.

What ultimately helps students excel in life is how they apply education to the real world. Life is a test that challenges people to look within to solve their issues. A whole person that has a spiritual nexus, an intelligent compass, and a well-rounded educative experience can rely on intellectual resources and foundational memory to guide and service their needs. Here is where spiritual faith relates and bonds with a person's education. Inevitably, the utilization of these tools better equips a person to overcome challenges while remaining focused to complete the journey.

Hip-hop is another strategic way to make use of intellectual resources and social capital to connect students to a school's curriculum. As a result, I have always utilized hip-hop as a subterfuge to connect literacy, social behavior, and racial consciousness to reverberate youth's awareness to contemporary issues.

Applying Cultural Value to a Hip-Hop Pedagogy

In what way does a cultural-relevant pedagogy (CRP) empower a hip-hop perspective? Essentially, a CRP model allows educators to listen to students' needs, address those needs, and connect an educator to a students' culture. Lessons within the classroom are tailored to support the community in a more meaningful way by adding their voice and cultural perspective to the instructional narrative (Billings, 2009). This model of teaching allows the educator to learn who the students are and relate the curriculum to their needs. What makes this an effective pedagogy is it provides youth with more options within a learning environment. Applying a hip-hop perspective to this pedagogy empowers young people's ability to navigate through a curriculum, integrating their experiences and social observations within an educational community. In particular, the usage of a CRP model incorporating a hip-hop modality in a literacy or social science course will increase minority students' level of engagement, classroom dialogue, and intellectual participation within the academic setting. Such a learning model further provides for minority youth a connecting bridge to school, because youth are better able to transfer their experiences, values, and perspectives to academic learning outcomes (Gillborn and Billings 2009).

According to researchers, a culturally relevant education model allows students to personalize their learning experiences while improving their perspective toward school (Perry, Steele, and Hillard III 2003). As a practice, when educators are able to construct a curriculum integrating hip-hop messaging, it presents meaning and value for young people. Students' cultural language, view, and perspectives from hip-hop only strengthen literacy and social science learning opportunities.

Literacy and Hip-Hop

A cultural toolkit's primary focus is to help youth actively respond and socially engage values, attitudes, and beliefs defining their families and communities. Reaffirming and challenging youth to interact and involve themselves into their community was the original precept of hip-hop. At first, the industry was largely misunderstood for its different fashion distinctions, values, and linguistic styles. Upon the cultural aspects of this industry taking positive roots into the community, many people began to view the empowering facets the music had on youth. From youths' involvement in exploring history, community development projects, and identity discovery, a new sense of awareness and consciousness was heightening through artistry presentations.

It was "cool," according to Boogie Down Productions, to investigate history to ascertain self-knowledge; it was necessary from the Jungle Brothers' perspective to pick up a "book to school yourself," and it was appropriate for a "brother to treat a sister like a queen" from the Brand Nubians concept of intellectual enlightenment (Brand Nubians 1998). The cornerstone to evoking this level of behavioral and cultural awareness was propagated through literacy. Reading as a cerebral activity equipped the rapper and listening audiences with strategies to socially engage and transform their environment. Illiteracy or the lack of knowledge would hinder a person's ability to develop strategies countering predatory individualism, activities, and hyper-materialism.

The importance of evoking literacy into the daily living routines and practices of a struggling community is nothing new. Books have always been a connective theme in liberation expression, thought, and action. For one, the text serves as an alternative to the experience and worldviews shaped by the dominant group. It also creates opportunities for oppressed cultural groups to examine and function outside the pejorative cultural domain (Freire 2000). In a unique way, literacy provides power to the voiceless while helping them develop opposing views to address their needs. Everyday living becomes transformed as individuals seek text as a tool to assess their predicament to define authentic realities.

Hip-hop was a resourceful tool that was used to include the voice and struggle of a people denied equitable opportunities within the system. Artists served as countervailing forces to portray a different level of expectations and beliefs regarding the conditions defining low-income groups. Prior to the corporatization of the experience, the definition of obtaining power did not rely on grandiose misogynist viewpoints, inflated macho egos, and oversized penises symbolized as a barrel of a gun. Rather, the voice of the artist, substantiated and supported through literacy, served as a viable resource to enlighten the inner workings of the soul about the dangers of buying into this sort of pathological perspective.

Hip-hop was once an educational source of information or cultural map that laid waste to all kinds of ignorance. For example, audiences experiencing this art form were told they were once kings and queens; they defined their own experiences, and they developed their own institutions. To validate this source of information, the names of text were "dropped" into ears to help create an intellectual dialogue of discovery and interaction. It was not surprising to find youth in the late 1980s and early '90s walking around with a book bag full of cultural text identifying them as historical investigators, racial critics, and community reformers.

The music also did not make youth fall short of learning and identifying with politics and how it develops imbalances of power, equity, and resource distribution. When Public Enemy pronounced, "While the devil takes care of makin' all the rules payin' mental rent, to corporate presidents (my man my man) ugh, one outta million residents bein' dissident, who ain't kissin' it. The politics of chains and whips got the sickness and chips and all the championships," it spoke to their frustrations and resentment toward unjust policy making (Public Enemy 98).

The deadly impact policies have on people of color is telling and speaks volumes to the way these imbalances affect minority communities. The message from this song further resonates the fact that economic and political success depends on people's level of involvement and activity to amend social conditions. Marginalized groups that do not defend, protect, or counter hegemony are doomed to "hell" by the oppressor, from Public Enemy's perspective. Political messaging such as this commands people to reject the status quo and work to make a social difference.

Counter Movement

When students acquire an instructional curriculum that successfully integrates their community, they are more apt to engage and mentally immerse themselves within the instructional pedagogy (Billings 2005). A teacher's ability to transfer hip-hop lyrics into their instructional practice shapes young people's awareness of current topics, political issues, or international dilemmas of the day. It also can serve to counter the anti-intellectualism pervading many social and cultural circles. Instead of listening and internalizing corporate rapper Rihanna's superficial, consumerist mentality, young people require more positive lyrical content rather than being informed to:

> Throw it up, throw it up/Watch it all fall out/Pour it up, pour it up/That's how we ball out/Throw it up, throw it up/Watch it all fall out/Pour it up, pour it up/That's how we ball out/Strip clubs and dollar bills/I still got my money/ Patron shots can I get a refill. (Rihanna 2012)

Through mass media's corporate appeal, youth are constantly encouraged to mimic "childlike," irresponsible adult behavior. Participating in conspicuous consumption while throwing what little money they possess into the air at a strip club instructs them to "splurge" on material items and adopt irresponsible financial behaviors.

As shown from Michele Alexander's work, current crime statistics and educational statistical data show that a "dumbed down," overly entertained minority population is a dangerous one (Alexander 2010; Postman 2005). Critical educators and social activists understand the harmful and persuasive influences this music has on young people, so they can develop critical pedagogy and strategies to neutralize the music's harmful message. In most minority communities, children as young as nine can be found listening to derogatory musical content before their arrival at school (Edmin 2010).

Educators and parents have to work harder deconstructing the harmful influences of this music. Without doing so, a serious form of conditioning continues to educate and teach youth how they should think and behave. On the contrary, when youth are fed intelligent critiques of society's structures, it counters the "dumbing down" syndrome funded by corporate zealots. Hip-hop has a legacy of educating and expanding youth's cultural knowledge, professional aspirations, and academic pursuits (Kitwana 2002).

When hip-hop listeners hear from Nas, they are encouraged to act and become an enlighten electorate population:

> I think Obama provides hope, and challenges minds/of
> all races and colors to erase the hate and try to *love* one
> another; so many political snakes/We in need of a break,
> I'm thinkin I can *trust* this brotha ... but will he keep it
> way real?/Every innocent nigga in jail, gets out on appeal/
> When he wins, will he really care still?" (Nas 2008)

Reviewing socially conscious hip-hop lyrics as part of a literacy strategy in the classroom is an effective way to encourage reading and writing reflective exercises. It further promotes students to critically engage in issues consuming their society.

The Trayvon Martin federal trial was the result of well-noted artist and activist working together to call attention to this serious issue. P-Diddy, Russell Simons, Jay-Z, and many others placed themselves into the social arena, funding and supporting activists such as Al Sharpton and Jessie Jackson to spur the federal government to reevaluate the state's case to not convict George Zimmerman (Clay 2012).

Despite the jury's decision, this encouraged a new hip-hop generation to fight back. An urgent sense of activism and post-civil rights collaboration emerged from this trial and several youth organizations were born. Where this goes remains to be seen; however, educators and activists must develop a similar partnership to further advance or add to this movement. A mobilized effort from responsible hip-hop artists and educators is an effective way to deconstruct corporate rap's negative messaging. Such positives will work to offset the serious amount of social apathy, irresponsible behaviors, and excessive consumerist mentalities translating far too many urban settings.

Instructional Vibrancy

When adopting a hip-hop culturally responsive pedagogy, the curriculum establishes an art-integrated practice because of the injection of creative auditory and visual stimuli into the academic setting. This helps connect students with the lessons being taught (Kitwana 2002). There exists vibrancy and "elastic impression" on students to relate to what the teacher is doing in the classroom when hip-hop emerges as part of the study or educational lesson. Several studies discussed by Hill, Emery, and Petchauer (2014) reviewed classroom cultures that infused lyrics into their literacy assignments. Students not only evaluated the context and inferences used from the lyrics, but also they were able to deconstruct the narrative or message delivered by the artist. Educators applying this practice of connecting students to literacy eventually align the information to required text or readings.

For example, educators can infuse the East and West Coast lyrical hip-hop rivalries into the study of literature by comparing them to Beowulf's boast poem of how this medieval epic hero victoriously defeated his adversary, Grendel.

When 2Pac declares in his song "Hail Mary" that
> I'm a ghost in these killin' fields/Hail Mary catch me if I go, let's go deep inside/The solitary mind of a madman who screams in the dark/Evil lurks, enemies, see me flee/Activate my hate, let it break, to the flame/ Set trip, empty out my clip, never stop to aim (2Pac 1996),

It sounds similar to the message in *Beowulf,* declaring that
> Death is not easily escaped/Try it who will/But every living soul among the children of men dwelling upon the earth goeth of necessity/Unto his destined place where the body/Fast in its narrow bed, sleepeth after feast. (British Literature 61)

Bringing together these passages allows an instructor to compare and contrast 2Pac's death premonitions with *Beowulf*'s epic battle eulogy

(Hill and Petchauer, 2014). The fact 2Pac's lyrics can be harnessed and used within the framework of a classroom environment supports the notion that learning is reciprocal and both a traditional and modern fabric of the past. Instructionally relating and connecting 2Pac lyrics to Old English, medieval literature, and ideas is intriguing enough to make supposedly challenged students relate to hip-hop machismo.

A hip-hop curriculum also provides teachers with the opportunity to utilize visual stimuli, which further promotes students' engagement with instructional lessons. Some teachers within urban school environments have been using hip-hop videos as "instructional hooks" to empower students' connection to their educational lessons (Smith, Jackson, Kitwana, and Pollard III 2012). For instance, students in a class on world history can refer to Lil Wayne's "God Bless Amerika" video to discuss how war and natural disasters are the leading factors causing refugee problems (Crawford 2014). Teachers can convey to students that people with minimal disposable resources are more deeply impacted by global tragedies.

To more effectively explain the instructional perspective, educators can display hip-hop video imagery of New Orleans' Lower Ninth Ward conditions in the aftermath of Hurricane Katrina. Using Lil Wayne's "God Bless Amerika" video would allow students to identify and explain the way poor African American Katrina victims were treated like refugees by their government similar to war refugees from Somalia or Serbia. The only difference is that Katrina victims encountered a disastrous flood from several levees collapsing, while civil war forced Somalian and Serbian people into destitute conditions.

When Lil Wayne (2013) says, "God bless Amerika, this so godless Amerika, I heard tomorrow ain't promised today, and I'm smoking on them flowers, catch the bouquet," while children in the video appear poor and hungry coming from deplorable housing conditions with an American flag draped as their landscape background, it communicates the notion that nobody cares about their suffering. When Lil Wayne raps that "Everybody wanna tell me what I need," and the condition hardly improves, it forces people to either "live by the sword and die by the sword" or better yet, smoke "weed" to mentally escape their living hell (Lil Wayne 2013; Jackson, Kitwana, and Pollard III 2012). Students residing in many poor urban communities completely identify with and relate to this video's message, and as a result they emphatically comprehend the lesson's objective. Similar to Lil Wayne, students discover the reality that Lower Ninth Ward residents share with Somalia and Serbian refugees. Furthermore, students can visually see how people in the Lower Ninth Ward have a second-class citizenship status parallel to poor people living in a third-world country.

Recall the day when the levees broke, leaving poor African Americans extremely vulnerable, and media outlets referred to these individuals as refugees (Horne, 2006). The hip-hop video lesson articulates for students their own experiences and challenges living within disadvantaged African American neighborhoods. A teacher's instruction becomes transformative when students are able to connect or relate an excitable "hip" video's imagery to lessons about world poverty and global disasters. This not only empowered students' voice and "buy in" to learn about global causes and effects defining a refugee, it provided a visual window of inescapable opportunity to synthesize the teacher's instructional motivation or intent.

Literacy Skills

The effective use of a hip-hop pedagogy builds on students' vocabulary pedigree and literary skills. Some curriculums are now applying hip-hop lyrics to translate literary poetic devices such as allusion, alliteration, kenning, or metaphors to advance students' comprehension of British English. When Romeo says to Juliet, "From forth the fatal loins of these two foes/A pair of star-crossed lovers take their life/Whose misadventure piteous overthrows/Doth with their death bury their parents," it applies the poetic device of allusion, comparable to Lupe's vernacular expression that, "Yeah, I am back up on the airwaves/Feeling like a soldier and I ain't talking where the Bears play/Flair, look how I Fred Astaire down the staircases/It's finna be a hair-raising tortoise versus hare race" (Lupe Fiasco 2006; Shakespeare 2014, 32). Many educators are applying hip-hop to teach poetry and classic literary works to engage students' focus toward such lessons.

Colloquial hip-hop expressions or words have also been used to advance the literary culture of America (Emdin 2010). It is ironic to find what was once thought of as "black slang" is now acceptable contemporary vernacular. Words like *flex, buggin', dope,* or *homie* are now part of our everyday linguistic terminology. Like a linguistic hyperbole, Americans are living in a time warp from the 1980s (Crawford 2014). Essentially, the hip-hop art form has helped many Americans discover their cultural linguistic self. When language is expressed as an art form, it better connects students to lessons and enriches a curriculum's objective (Delpit 2006).

There are multiple ways hip-hop can communicate language by shifting different terms to translate a message. If applied to instruction, students could decode traditional English into their own cultural message. In other words, hip-hop vocabulary is used to create a new reality with the way students accurately understand and describe their comprehension of classroom lessons.

Lisa Delpit and Theresa Perry (2006), and Claude Steele and Asa Hilliard III (1998) discuss how cultural language should advance the educational experience to provide students with a better opportunity to express their understanding and synthesis of subject matter. This model actually facilitates higher-learning experiences within the classroom because students speak and interpret from a perspective of instructional understanding. It increases students' involvement and participation within the learning arena. Some critics suggest this model is nothing more than the Ebonics debate, whereby people argue that students learn better if allowed to speak from their native dialect or tongue. Ebonics is critiqued as simply bad language by those who profess to represent the vanguard of applying appropriate forms of communication of the English language. Words such as *shortie, peeps,* and *da* are not only viewed as offensive colloquial expressions but are referenced as dysfunctional modicums of expression. However, a culturally values-driven pedagogy stresses the importance of educators allowing students to utilize their cultural dialect in academic spaces to effectively communicate their ideas and comprehensive expression of instructional lessons. To do so inevitably grants minority learners with more access to engage academia. (Perry and Delpit 1998).

Similarly, some scholars believe this language's conceptual model incapacitates students' ability to translate the standard language system into academic and professional success. Such an argument has been widely addressed for a number of years. Hip-hop linguistics critically contradicts this argument, supporting the viewpoint that students learn better when they speak and translate conversations from their own realities.

When students are translating and decoding instruction from their lens, Delpit (2006) refers to this type of learning as *biculturality*. This means students have a language system of their own that requires valuing and adherence if learning is to actually take place within a standard classroom setting. When this occurs, a classroom becomes authenticated and real, because students are intellectually qualifying academic concepts based on their linguistic understanding (Perry, Steele, and Hilliard 2003).

Restoring a Connection

A hip-hop CRP model allows students' inner human and cultural experiences to materialize within the physical space of a classroom. When students are provided opportunities of self-expression, they are educated to learn how classroom instruction connects with their own lived experiences and environments. Rapper KRS-One expounds on this, saying, "This, of course, is in no way a degradation of math and science. But if math and science are not put in their proper intellectual places, real *hip-hop* as well as the nature of one's true reality will be impossible to comprehend" (Parker 17). Math and science, according to KRS-One, as authentic sciences, should be used to help students perceive the importance of learning these brilliant pedagogies rather than believing they are somehow obscure or disconnected experiences. Math is used every day when, for example, spending money or thinking about how to access power; whereas, science assists in cooking or nourishing one's body. In other words, both of these fields have to be applied and shown to students to demonstrate how they contribute to their intellectual wherewithal.

When students perceive learning as a part of their reality, it causes them to want to learn more. The problem, from Paulo Freire's (2000) belief, is that far too many subject areas are taught as an abstract concept instead of an applied approach. History, science, math, and English are viewed as separated fragments of each other rather than interdisciplinary units of the same field. All of these subjects should be utilized and connected to students' educational experiences by way of project based learning opportunities. Whatever learners are currently studying in history should already apply to what they are learning in English, science, and math. Freire asserts this is a type of classical education where fields of study are seen as organic experiences versus an abstract study.

KRS-One addresses this issue when he teaches about the origins of hip-hop as a cultural movement from his lectures and published work. As it relates to history, KRS-One discusses Afrika Bambaataa's architecture and engineering of a cultural movement that blended math, science, and English. From the standpoint of cleaning up or redeeming parts of New York's urban culture that had been abandoned by mainstream society, Bambaataa used music as a source to teach people how they could transform their lives. Embedded within this musical narrative is a powerful lesson of how people used graffiti or "tagging" to beautify abandoned, burnt-out apartment complexes scattered throughout the Bronx and Brooklyn that were deliberately destroyed by arsonist landlords to collect insurance claims. To exorcise illicit and criminal activities normalized within these abandoned buildings' interiors and courtyards, Bambaataa produced and performed at parties (Parker 2013). As an English lesson, poetry with its multiple literary devices educated and entertained people about their cultural history and the principles of community empowerment. Rent parties emerged to support families in need. Aesthetic graffiti became a necessary tool to manifest innate natural talents to reclaim forgotten spaces. Disc jockeys like Kool DJ Herc and Grand Master Flash engineered their record turntables, applying science and math, using thrown away mechanical parts from industrial lots and janitorial garbage to develop the "cut and scratch" dual technique of playing music. Hip-hop, to become a success, applied an interdisciplinary methodology to proactively engage its clientele and community. It changed the way today's youth self-express their attitudes and behaviors in the classroom or neighborhoods where they live. An interdisciplinary project-based CRP construct must be come formatted to create an effective intellectual fervor in youth to empower their experiences in the classroom. Without orchestrating a direct, interdisciplinary response to students, they will continue to remain disengaged, disconnected, and unexpressed within many standard classroom settings.

Constructing an Engaging Pedagogy

With the emergence of a common-core curriculum in public schools, there is an opportunity to integrate cultural relevant materials to engage urban youth. Despite the over-amount of testing and instructional scrutiny attached to this curriculum, it presents an opportunity for educators to teach cultural literacy and emerging concepts to improve learners' academic skills. Examples of such practices are shown in several school settings where teachers are developing project-based assessments presenting relevant concepts (e.g., Hip-Hop Education project, Hip-Hop Academy, Mobilized 4 Movement project) (Asante 2009; Fernandes 2011). Students in their classes are taught how to research academic journals, create community-based projects, publish their writing, and complete English and social studies interdisciplinary tasks. Teachers construct youth-empowerment activities in their classrooms to heighten students' cultural competency and problem-solving skills, which enhance their critical reading and writing proficiency (Edmin 2010). More importantly, students are engaged in classroom lessons that uphold cultural principles, best-practice approaches, and behavioral practices that advance urban communities. At the Baltimore Performing Arts High School and Harvard University there is a course titled Tupac Shakur's Hip-hop Pedagogy, where students apply literary rhyming schemes reading and writing in the style of Shakespeare (Asante 2009). The hip-hop principles of Whodini's *One Love* and Nas' *One Mic and The World is Ours* is used to influence educators, staff, administrators, and community members to engage societal concerns. In addition, students are made to embrace, connect with, and display positive beliefs and attitudes. The results are students within a hip-hop curriculum who transform into cultural and intellectual capitalist, which leads them to excel beyond the required standard requirements. Ultimately, an infusion of a hip-hop curriculum imposes symbiotic connections between educators, learners, and communities to deconstruct racial stereotypes, misogyny, and cultural divisions.

PART IV

"Can You Stand the Rain?"

Corporate Flood

Rain levels have been picking up and increasing for more than a few months in Chicago and outlying areas of the city. It is now April 2013, and flood warnings along with weather reports forecast the region's doom as nearby streams, ponds, and rivers overflow into the basements of homes and residential communities. "Warning ... this is not a drill!" captivates the listening audience's attention, informing them to evacuate their communities because levees and riverbeds can no longer hold the onslaught of water headed toward their doors. Restless, survival-minded populations of residents flee with a few of their possessions to seek alternative shelter to escape nature's wrath upon their community. Where they will go or what they will return to has yet to be clearly answered.

Welcome to the wonderful world of education, where severe rainfall represents the sweeping changes caused by school privatization; emergency warnings signal the government sanctioning of urban school reform; and students, parents, and educators struggle to abandon their school community-epitomized evacuees.

If this analogy appears farfetched regarding contemporary school reform, think again. Many well-established, traditional school models throughout the nation are forced to close because they do not meet the educational expectations and standards of society—or so we are led to believe. Diane Ravitch (2010) suggests private investors and developers view current schoolhouses as marketable places for commerce transactions, development, and entrepreneurship. In hindsight, struggling schools challenged with the perplexity to improve their performance are saddled with the obvious statement of resentment: "You will either improve your scores or we will shut you down!" Ravitch further argues corporate venture capitalists' last market cornered is education. Prior to education, all other major global institutions and markets have been exploited or conquered by Adam Smith's vision of a free-market society. As a result, urban schools are under siege with reforms generated from philanthropists enthused with improving education while buttressing their stock portfolio.

Historically speaking, this is not a new concept established by the elite. According to Watkins in *The White Architects of Black Education* (2001), philanthropists of the late 1800s post-Civil War-era found an

75

inescapable need to develop structures that controlled and shaped the norms and values of African American society; moreover, they deemed it their duty to establish a curriculum that advanced the industrial era.

During the early part of the twentieth century, a new age of schools configured society's landscape as philanthropist developed educational models that reflected their business and behavioral expectations. The statement that says, "The more things seem to change, the more they remain the same" reflects what is happening in education today. Venture capitalists from the Waltons to the Gates have discovered effective ways to invest and translate their wealth into America's economy. The only difference being educators of the nineteenth and twentieth centuries implemented and designed schools tailored to policymakers' vision of quality education, whereas today, school reform is largely based on corporate business standards of finished product and yield returns (Watkins 2011). Paula Lipman (2011) expands this perspective, suggesting urban markets are "rife" for innovation and transformation due to economic decay and years of infrastructural neglect. Similar to a war-torn community in Afghanistan or Iraq, "Educational Halliburton" is delving out contracts left and right to private investors, promising to turn around failing public schools in five years.

Traditional schools that once existed fifty to a hundred years in urban spaces are now replaced with charter-contract schools promising to produce improved results from children of color. How effective these schools will improve minorities' educational position remains to be seen. However, what we do know is for more than ten years of No Child Left Behind and *Race to the Top,*

- the white and black achievement gap remains high;
- minority suspension rates particularly of African American and Latino males have widened;
- the African American teaching forces have been severely reduced;
- teacher and administrative retention rates have declined; and
- separate and unequal school structures flourish throughout urban America's promised land (Ravitch 2014).

To claim that these pressing issues should have declined in ten years is an unrealistic expectation. However, it appears very little has changed in the way schools are managed in contemporary America.

Administrative Exodus

After leaving my second high school job, my next stop was administration. Here I learned about what truly takes place behind the scenes of the schools. Not only is administration very political, but a person discovers the business side driving education. My new job title was curriculum coordinator, a fancy way to say instructional coach. My mission, intent, and purpose were to help teachers construct lessons that were meaningful, relevant, and aligned to college readiness standards. My new employment location took me out of the city limits into a middle-class community in the south suburbs of Chicago. From what I learned prior to taking this job, the district's most recent influx of Chicago African American migrants challenged the educational model at its core. Teacher struggled with managing their classrooms, delivering and applying quality instructional practices, and properly assessing the cultural needs of student. More importantly, test results drastically declined, transitioning this school community from a blue ribbon model to a second-tier school. I was not taken aback by such disparate indifference within the district because it was a phenomenon that usually swept across demographically shifted communities.

Once upon a time after the *Brown v. Board of Education* Act in 1954, during the 1960s and '70s, transforming neighborhoods experienced severe racial turmoil that impacted school districts' ability to effectively instruct students of color. Inevitably, many white residents moved out of such neighborhoods to escape school integration while seeking homogenized communities to regain their former living experience. Businesses, resources, and investment capital followed behind these residents as they ran away deeper and further away from their African American citizens. Scholars termed this "white flight"; I refer to it as "outer-core exodus," a term coined by Michael Foucault (1994) to describe how suburban whites extended city limits a second time post-World War II to escape incoming minority residents. Outer-core exodus also refers to whites' navigation or manifest destiny to seek communities not connected or outside of a minority's spatial sphere. As a result, they push further and further beyond human terrain to escape any sort of relationship with people of color.

It is also no surprise that when economic infrastructure leaves a community, the resources, schools, and development will decline. Prior to my arrival to the school district, for about twenty years the south suburban school district underwent this ethnographic phase shift, which led to many unique social challenges and political turmoil. Racially speaking, by the time I arrived, the school district's student populations was majority African American; however, the teacher population was approximately 80 percent white. I already suspected as much upon taking my new job. With my arrival came the district's first African American superintendent, school board members, a few more teachers, two black male principals, and a curriculum coordinator. To say such change would cause some teacher resentment is an understatement. The district was now navigating through some tough racial waters, which would test everyone's mental and spiritual mantle.

My duty was clear: help teachers support minority learners struggling within their classrooms, provide educators with research-based strategies to instructionally engage and challenge students, and improve the district's reading scores. I just so happened to work at a school within the district incurring steep racial divisions, parent resentment, and low teacher morale. Despite these challenges, I made it my goal to work with the parents, teachers, and administrators to improve the school's collegial and cultural environment. The problem with this goal was that I had no clue how to actually successfully perform such an arduous task. I referenced my own research along with several others, most notably Ogbu, Billings, and Sergiovanni.

As a first-year administrator working alongside social studies teachers, I believed I could shower them with enough support and input to improve reading within the school. In hindsight or as a "yesteryear afterthought," I wish I had applied several distinct techniques prior to doling out responsibilities, expectations, or demands.

First, I should have had a sit down with union leaders to inform them about the plans, goals, and vision I had toward improving our department's reading scores. Second, I should have developed a close relationship with the English curriculum coordinator to align and develop new strategies to teach reading in the department. This would have meant having monthly joint professional development sessions to have freshmen, sophomore, junior, and senior teachers grouped to design a curriculum that met the needs of the students while integrating our instructional lessons. In addition, I would have loved to see some team-building exercises and co-teaching between our departments, especially when literacy-text supported the content and skills delivered in the classroom. Mapping out interdisciplinary units, exercises, and activities would have helped enrich the culture and collegiality at our school.

However, what occurred was totally different from what I envisioned happening. First and foremost, departments worked within location of each other and rarely aligned their curriculum. Also, the teacher union was incredibly strong and seemed to resist any changes not reviewed by their leaders. However, I sometimes felt they were too overprotective of poor-performing instructors. Today, I deeply understand their aims and intent. It truly was not a matter of questioning our strategies but rather the curriculum implementation and procedural expectations of supporting new school policy. With such wide and varied change, union members may have felt like we were out to get them. Nothing was further from the truth, especially with my position, since I taught a few classes alongside my colleagues that helped me relate to their concerns and challenges. Not to mention I believed we could map out strategies that effectively improved the performance of African American learners.

Instead, what I received from most educators working in this environment was a whole lot of resentment, stigma, and sublime misunderstanding. Like most of my administrative colleagues believed, a line was drawn between educators. This made the climate incredibly poor and troubling as we attempted to improve student performance.

Parent relationships were also deplorable with the school community. To ensure parents understood my intent, I held several meetings with the parent president and community members. They expressed outrage and contempt toward specific practices and policies, which they asserted caused more harm toward their children. To improve parent relationships within the school, I made it a point to set up monthly meetings, involve parents in our school-related activities, sponsor and organize a history club, and visit classrooms.

What I received from establishing this partnership was complete outrage from union heads along with several teachers. Indirectly, my principal made it a point to communicate that I needed to stay away from specific parents; otherwise she could not protect me from union harassment. At this point I became disenchanted, expecting more from my leader. However, my idealistic resolve would not allow me to give up on my vision to establish a quality relationship with parents. Without parental support or community involvement, a school will only go so far to make its attempted gains. Research time and time again supports the importance of parental involvement in a school's learning environment. My thinking was why not make the parents part of the learning community in such a way they help us patrol the hallways, mentor students, serve as volunteer support staff to teachers, and mediate disciplinary infractions? It was this type of thinking that caused major challenges for me within the learning environment. My friendly relationship and connection to parents eventually caused my transition from this climate. From monitoring my office visits, hallway movements, and indirect and direct communication with teachers, I was "policed" every day to coerce my transition from the school.

Despite my professional ordeals, I was able to accomplish several major feats at the school. First, I charted a school community-parent based program titled Cultural Film-Literacy Series. This program was originally created to increase parent and student involvement in our district's social science department. What emerged were greater parent collaborations and participation in our social science's events, activities, and outings. The cultural film-literacy series successfully did several things:

(1) historical presentation of documentaries promoted social activism and cultural awareness in the community;

(2) A book-of-the-month club surfaced, which led to literacy round-table discussions and author presentations;

(3) Financial donations and grant proposals supported student travel or school sponsored field trips, and

(4) A guest-speaker series of prominent scholastic and social figures visited our social science classrooms, conducted school

assemblies, and were attendees at the film-literacy sessions. Today, the program continues to manage its efforts to include parents' and students' active participation in the district's social science department.

Another great professional achievement I enacted was developing a male and female mentor program that engaged minorities to abide by the norms, policies, and procedures of the school community. The program's basic tenets were to enrich social interactions and connections with students who struggled in education; motivate and connect their interest in school; and incorporate a value-cultural relevant framework to help them learn the importance of school achievement. Providing students with enriched experiences while connecting them to successful role models from the community truly helped advance their social behavior, cultural context, and intellectual sophistication. The success of the program continues to nourish, replenish, and reenergize students to prepare them to live life in a productive and well-rounded manner.

Clearly, my community service and parental connections were indeed strong. However, I struggled to establish those same relationships with educators working in the learning environment. Initially, I always believed it was a result of my color line. On the other hand, I could have done things differently to establish an improved rapport with my teaching colleagues. This, of course, means mistakes were made along the way during my administrative experience. Lack of mentoring and intervention and the district's vision made it damn near impossible to understand. Notwithstanding, the aforementioned elements are essential to produce effective leadership. Besides the superintendent pulling me aside at various intervals of the day to conduct a moment of noteworthy and strategic reflections, I felt like everyone else was just waiting for me to fail. Such an attitude and disposition made going to work became a chore. Hell! I almost quit after three months into this stressful job but was talked out of it by my former principal, who encouraged me to stick with it for a year. It became clear to me that I had to focus on student and parent connections and work to improve the climate and culture within my department. Whatever it took, I felt a need to focus my energy toward forming congenial partnerships between parents, students, and social science faculty members. Besides battling certain union and administrative figureheads, healthy relationships would add value and meaning to my work. Ultimately, I hoped this energy would spread to other departments to serve as a blueprint for what should be occurring within our building.

After two years of working in the district, I was exhausted. No amount of energy manifested through students, parents, and a few of my social studies colleagues would be enough for me to continue this administrative journey. The issues of low-test performance, poor teacher morale, volatile parent interactions, and a resentful union convinced me why I had to make an exodus.

What shamed me about my experience was the amount of low performing and academic expectations leveled toward African American students. As previously mentioned, the majority of the district's learners came from very productive and stable home environments with a middle-class economic status, yet their academic achievement was similar to poor students attending a low-performing urban high school. In addition, the issues that surfaced in the dean's office reminded me of the behavioral ordeals I encountered at my previous high school.

Unfortunately, too many parents were either enabling their child's behavior or blamed teachers for ineffective classroom management. More disturbing, it appeared parents rewarded their children with material goods to compensate for their lack of constructive time or emotional attention. Parents were constantly working to provide the suburban "Promised Land" to their children, which diminished their opportunity to effectively bond or emotionally build with them. The end result was parents who supported and backed their children when they were totally wrong. Of course this is not unique or indifferent to the district; as school case scenarios and counseling reports suggest across America's educational landscape, parents are exhibiting the same type of behavioral interactions. Poor relationships between the community, parents, and teachers helped drive a wedge between those appropriately disciplining learners who were "out of control" and those who wanted to ignore the behavior.

Even further, teachers struggled with properly diagnosing disrespectful behavior. A lot of this has had a great deal to do with teachers not being trained to adhere to a cultural responsive curriculum, which would have helped alleviate a great deal of the indifferences shaping this district's climate. To appease parents and attempt to develop a sensible relationship with them, administrators compromised their policies, which did not support or back educators. This resulted in or led to further distrust and despair from classroom instructors. If they could not effectively discipline students or enforce their classroom norms, how could they possibly teach disruptive and disrespectful learners?

John Ogbu's book *Black Americans Students in an Affluent Suburb* (2003) explores the performance of learners in Shaker Heights, Ohio. Ogbu's analysis and investigation revealed African American learners differed no better than the average poor learner at an underperforming school. Spoiled from the privileges of upward mobility and post-Civil Rights gains, a number of learners were rarely taught to appreciate the educational opportunities and resources readily made available to them. Consequently many learners within the school district neglected their studies, which resulted in low level of performance. Ogbu made mention of several major problems impacting student's performance:

- ineffective parent support systems,
- adherence to a subculture code that countered traditional norms,
- a deficit student work ethic,
- a limited cultural responsive curriculum,
- poor communication between staff and parents,
- pacification and embracement of limited expectations, and
- inconsistent appropriation and administering of policy.

Parents not only publicly supported and excused their children's lack of academic effort, they blamed educators for students' limited initiative. Ogbu asserted the Shaker Heights School District would have been better equipped to handle and address this challenge through

- developing an alignment of policy implementation between the school community and parents, which would establish and clarify curriculum expectations;
- constructing cultural workshops, seminars, and forums to train and prepare faculty members to develop a responsive curriculum approach;

- integrating or infusing parents into the social fabric and environment of the school community (e.g., student volunteers, mediators, ambassadors);
- increasing the level of academic expectations and requirements for students;
- hiring more well-trained African American faculty members to become positive identifiers and models for students, and
- promoting effective support mechanisms for teachers struggling within the learning environment.

Ogbu concludes educators should never discount the amount of impact parents can achieve toward advancing quality schooling. To discount or discredit parents is to destroy a school community. Often the case, parents require the same amount of education and support as learners to understand school goals, district expectations, and policies. Otherwise, most parents will cater to the needs of their children over the expectations of a school's learning environment. Armed with this information, I understood the importance of providing our parents with a specific set of roles within the social science department.

State assessment scores continue to drop lower and lower, demonstrating a disjointed alignment between state standards and the district's curriculum goals. Again, this continues to surface and remain a major challenge in most American high schools. Most teachers worked incredibly hard to engage students while designing creative lessons. However, the teachers who surrendered or gave up on quality instruction were either "burned out," embraced low expectations, or were too comfortable with their teaching practice.

Similar to parents protecting their "unruly kids," unionized educators fared no better rushing to the defense of their colleagues to protect their job. Administrators had to jump through hoops to attempt to dismiss an ineffective teacher, especially a tenured-track faculty member. Therefore, many administrators pacified union school officials by allowing ineffective educators to remain in the classroom. The result: administrators believed their hands and feet were tied or stifled between the realities of working with or against classroom teachers.

To solve this problem, many school districts have disposed of unions by developing non-union member charter schools. However, this does not address or solve the challenges many districts have with establishing an effective relationship with educators. Anytime administrators can terminate an educator without due process or limited professional feedback promotes a level of intolerance and toxic distrust. Effective teachers have a democratic right to be protected, supported, and properly treated; on the other hand, ineffective teachers should not receive the same degree of assurances.

These issues almost forced me out of the educational profession. I desperately needed a hiatus to nurture my professional spirit. I resigned at the end of my two-year tenure to head back to the classroom. I took a tremendous pay cut leaving this job to rediscover and reset my passion for teaching and learning. Indeed, I was disappointed I had failed to deliver the type of effective leadership that would transform the district's performance, yet I could celebrate some accomplishments and positive aspects about my experience. In the end, my best work had yet to be completed as I journeyed back to the classroom.

For the Love of Money

Chicago closed more than fifty-plus schools, from what the public has been told, to save the city's budget from unnecessary expenditure cost for sites deemed under-enrolled, failing, or physically unfit to service students. Despite union and parent protest, public scrutiny, and mixed bipartisan reviews regarding Chicago public schools closures, several newly emerging charter-contract schools have surfaced. The message is clear: traditional public schools experiencing low achievement, limited resources, and troubled enrollment will no longer exist within the city.

Chicago and New York radically appear to represent the new standard for public schooling across the nation. In years past, philanthropic and policy efforts emphasized a need to fund and stabilize troubled schools in challenged neighborhoods. However, school closures today demonstrate a different direction in terms of how education will become funded and maintained. There is so much capital and financial net gain to be had by private investors, the last space for capitalist developers to exploit, there is no way they plan to expend money toward schools deemed failing. For them, it would be like throwing money away. So why not invest in schools that appear improved while at the same time have the ability to dispose or hire employees, improve contracting and business opportunities, and obtain various state and federal resources to direct schools. When looking at the raw numbers shaping school budgets or the net worth of education, public school buildings compose a great deal of a city's workforce, business infrastructure, and contract investment (Ravitch 2014).

By average, a local schoolhouse manages three to five million dollars annually (Lipman 2011). If no longer in the hands of the public or taxpayers, investors obtain an amicable deal handling a school. First and foremost, the paying public continues to shell out taxes to support charter or contract schools governed by a private service provider. This affords them the chance to create more funding from state and federal coffers to support the development of a school.

Second, there exists very little oversight or regulation as to how they manage school budgets or resources disseminated to their educational arenas. Next, school contracts are varied and multifaceted as investors choose from a wide selection of vendors and resources readily available. From deciding paper and book distributors to determining food services and building construction, a considerable amount of money becomes obtainable in the world of education.

Finally, private developers are changing the way school curriculums are constructed and taught to students, making it all the more enjoyable to design assessment tools and products to service students. Indeed, schools are the new cash cow for developers in a collapsing, overly recessed economy. To successfully push this new school approach, it became important that policyholders, corporate entities, and investors shared a critical commonality: destroying unions while changing urban space to ensure capital returns.

UNO, a private charter school development located in Illinois and situated on the west side of Chicago, most recently received a private grant and state funding to build a new school. The funding was legislated and passed in 2010 to forward more than thirty million dollars to not only design a new building but to create an innovative education approach

(Catalyst Chicago 2014). Despite some protest from local vendors and school officials, UNO was rewarded state capital to develop and expand their school operations. The administrative heads and corporate investors of UNO were well-received and congratulated for capturing state and local funds to continue their development of schools. Not to mention the taxpaying public would continue to pay for schools either out of district or outside public control to support the increase of a private school unit.

Similar to private owners that own excessively large stadiums, school owners are the latest kids on the block, so to speak, with no recourse or affiliation to public interest (Zirin 2013). Current owners develop massive stadiums at the public's expense to manage their private teams to service the entertaining value of the public. Of course they offer a product to the public that invests in it while believing it provides a needed value to their interest.

However, the public does not own the team, reap the financial rewards or capital gains from the franchise, or receive a large amount of the contracts doled out to developers or vendors. Rather, they pay for stadiums that continue to dig financial holes and burdens into the taxpaying public while bridges, schools, roads, and essential health services crumble before their eyes. Ironically, some of these franchises are inferior and do not deserve the amount of incredible financial incentives and support they receive (e.g., Chicago Bears). Yet investors understand their worth and do not hesitate to fund stadiums and private sport facilities that garner a tremendous amount of profits. How different is this from private charters or school organizations seeking to reform a school system?

As Chicago continues to close public schools down, they are opening several new charter and contract schools. Increasingly so, school budgets continue to evaporate as policyholders and government officials declare their state and local municipalities are broke (Ravitch 2014). Despite this, Chicago has approved of two new stadium deals to direct millions of dollars versus forwarding funding to public schools achieving state benchmarks and district requirements to retain teachers, support staff, and instructional services. Of course, this has now become an identifiable problem because white students mostly north of the city are affected from this economic policy decision.

Meanwhile, the Chicago Cubs are frantically fighting over tax dollars and state funding to expand Wrigley Field; whereas, DePaul University has been promised a new state-of-the-art stadium at Navy Pier. Despite the state and city being busted for funds, they are shelling out multimillion-dollar contracts and streamlined revenue to support new stadiums and private schools. Why? Because they reap considerable profits for investors and owners while increasing revenue for the city. This proves public schools are thought to be a drain on society, especially prevalent in communities ravaged with crime, despair, and mostly minorities.

The thought is: Why continue to shift depleted public funds into schools not yielding a bottom line; paying salaries for educators not sufficiently achieving specific state results; and investing in dilapidated buildings that require large sums of money to rehabilitate? Similar to sports owners suffering from an itch to build a new stadium or threatening to relocate their team if taxpayers do not fund their private franchise, school organizations like UNO understand the profits to be had investing in public education.

Not surprisingly, UNO was investigated for mismanaging its state contracts, underpaying workers, practicing nepotism when hiring vendors and construction workers, and misappropriating the direction of public funds. As a result, the state rescinded their contract and state grant that hurt the organization's ability to manage several of their charter schools (Catalyst Chicago 2014). The president of the charter organization, versus resigning like any moral politician would do, decided to apologize for being caught by the state and promised to restructure its organization and financial handlings. Eventually, the state renewed UNO's funding and promised to investigate and review charter organizations with more scrutiny.

How many charter organizations or schools exist similar to UNO where they are provided an indiscriminate amount of autonomy and limited oversight to manage public funds? Several well-known charter organizations across the United States have been busted and closed for failing to deliver quality educational services, mismanaging public resources, and contracting partiality (Lipman 2011). The results are that millions of dollars have been siphoned from phony investors viewing children, communities, and educators as economic reserves.

Stanford University reported that several charter schools in California, Pennsylvania, Texas, and Ohio were found to have school CEOs taking money from their own schools, putting unqualified relatives on their payrolls, and engaging in other questionable activities (Cohen 2015).

Even worse, nineteen of the seventy-four charter schools operating in Philadelphia are under investigation for fraud, financial mismanagement, and conflicts of interest. In many ways, these new school reforms are no more effective than the traditional plans of yesteryear. Far too many urban schools continue to remain segregated, there remains no significant changes with the learning gap between whites and blacks. Besides schools existing as community hubs and public investments, they now are assigned to private purveyors to restructure them to make a profit for the goodwill of the people.

To effectively develop new schools while at the same time attracting private investors, urban zones or spaces have to improve (Lipman 2011). This means specific communities require gentrification to restore investor confidence when developing new school structures. Communities almost have to become sanitized or restructured to support a new school. Otherwise, private investors do not believe there is financial value supporting an improved school arrangement. Coincidentally, this has caused metropolitans like Chicago to simply close multiple schools down because the neighborhoods require too much work to transform. The result is communities that are left to die rather than invested in to maintain their existence; indeed, this also includes schools that struggle to function in disadvantage communities. Again, the idea is to shut them down instead of supporting their existence. This reportedly saves money, time, and effort to progress a school deemed too difficult to restructure. It also creates for the city, state, and federal government a chance to redirect funds in a skillful way to better facilitate expenditure cost and financial capital. Turning over responsibilities to private investors is an effective way for them to save money, restore the public's confidence in education, and shift populations in urban zones. However, the effectiveness of such a new policy and direction has yet to benefit majority of minority public school children. Despite the success stories of charter schools improving the educational needs of students, far too many underperform and academic accounts remain similar to traditional public models.

My Schoolhouse Is a Ghost Town

Returning to the classroom brought about a tremendous amount of joy and relief because it was here where the soul of teaching rested. I discovered a new sense of purpose teaching history again in front of learners excited to discover unknown facts, events, and philosophies defining their existence.

However, upon my return to a newly formed art contract school, I discovered the pedagogical model had shifted from a teacher-driven skill-based model to an assessment-driven instructional construct. No longer could I tailor lessons to a sustentative content analysis, historical interpretation, and literacy fact extrapolation; instruction had to relate to a heavy Eurocentric ACT standard framework. In many ways, history or social science had become another reading class driven behind standards that taught to the test. This made history seem fleeting and nonessential because students would not become challenged to view the relevancy and practicality of the past. Not to mention the fact students would struggle to analyze how contemporary ordeals are configured by cultural and historical legacies. What I further discovered was quite a number of schools had eliminated history courses outright or referred to it as humanity studies, a fused composition of English and social sciences. History was no longer necessary if it did not align with reading selections presented on the state assessment. I questioned whether I would be able to abide by these new sets of standards.

The school was a brand-new model formed by the Chicago Public School District and major art partners. The school would exist as Chicago's first public performing art establishment. While art budgets and programs were being cut out of many traditional schools, Chicago decided to develop a contract school that catered to the artistic needs of students. From music, visual arts, dance, and theater students were taught pre-professional skills to work in the world of art. So much research indicates the positive effects of art influences on student development, achievement, and creativity. Despite many schools and students having a limited ability to participate in such wonderful programs, learners at this location were afforded new opportunities to study and receive artistic training. It cost the district millions of dollars to develop this school as they closed other public schools down, eliminating art programs. Teachers were hired as at-will employees with no union, a lower pay scale, and limited financial incentives. In other words, an instructor could be let go at any time within the school year without recourse.

This was a little frightening for me, because I realized education was officially undergoing a new phase of instruction employing teachers and managing schools. It also became clearer that teachers, regardless of the school environment, community challenges, or student needs were held to the exact evaluation and standards to produce quality test scores, high graduation rates, and high school attendance. The message resonated for teachers working within these newly formed environments that accountability was extremely high to achieve specific results the district deemed acceptable. Why on earth would I seek to return to a school designed under these arrangements negating my tenure, pension, and security? Quite honestly, I had little choice in the matter as a teacher in Chicago. Most of the schools were either closing, enrollment was decreasing, or performance was terrible.

Attempting to function in a traditional school was challenging due to a number of constraints, particularly:

- If a teacher attempted to find employment or reassignment to a new school coming from a failing one, chances of receiving employment was slim to none. Educators working in such schools were viewed as poor instructors, despite their success, competency, and credentials;
- Schools tended to hire new teachers with limited experience and few credentials so they did not have to pay them at a high rate. Veteran teachers were now declared too expensive, established, and philosophically resistant to the structural shifts occurring within the district;
- Budget cuts had eliminated many teaching and administrative positions in public schools, which caused educators with limited experience to lose their jobs. The employment field

doubled because there were plenty of competent and highly qualified instructors out of work; and

- Teacher unions were viewed as a threat or imposition to newly formed standards and schools. For years, the business world and policyholders informed the taxpaying public the teacher unions were the main culprit behind students' poor results and deficiencies because they protected bad teachers. To counter this, new schools employed tactics discouraging the creation and development of an organized union.

As a result, two spheres existed within the system: non-union or union schools. If a teacher came from a strong, unionized school, it diminished his or her chances of being hired into a contract or charter arrangement.

The one advantage I had attempting to become hired as an instructor was that I had recently came from an administrative position external to the district for a few years. In addition, a collegiate acquaintance knew the principal and strongly recommended me for the position. The school was seeking a few veteran teachers to mix and balance their hiring pool of new teachers. This assisted my efforts and abilities to acquire a teaching position within the school. Again, I was concerned by the new standards imposed by the system and sought a convenient way to change my teaching assignment within the school.

An epiphany asserted itself for me working at the new school because the building once existed as Douglass Elementary. In fact, I attended Douglass for preschool growing up down the street. Teaching here created glimpses of my childhood past as I walked the halls and discovered an old room I once sat and learned in. Douglass exists no more because a new elementary and high school had taken its place. There was so much history about Douglass I needed to share with my students, but it would not align with the new standards appearing on a state test. For one, Douglass was named after Senator Stephen Douglass, a famous senator from Illinois who believed in the idea of popular sovereignty, which meant new territories or states should vote to decide if they wanted slavery to exist; whereas, Abraham Lincoln, an opposing candidate running for the senate seat believed slavery posed a moral question to states and the union (Bennett 1993). Second, the site was once a federal prison war camp for confederate soldiers. Confederates were held at Camp Douglass approximately three years, from 1862 to 1865. Lastly, the location is a famous historical Native American burial ground. Every year, Native Americans hold a prayer ritual honoring their ancestors' remains at this site.

In many ways, this school held a considerable amount of history and legacy for students, but neither the administration or the board of education cared. This is when I realized my former schoolhouse was a ghost town. How many more ghost towns existed throughout the city where schools' histories and communities were shut down or removed?

A number of schools were being wiped away from the pages of history similar to the way western railroad tracks displaced Native Americans from their indigenous lands. In fact, a recent study surfaced in Chicago indicating majority of the schools shut down are named after famous African Americans (Catalyst Chicago 2012).

So much history shaped and defined school communities helping to construct Chicago's legacy, how could policyholders and business leaders simply do away with it as though it never existed? Schools that once existed for more than one hundred years, with the history of the first African American migrants to the north, are now shuttered or broken into two or three smaller charter school units.

Diane Ravitch (2014) strongly believes public schools will not improve if cities continue to close neighborhood schools in the name of reform. She argues neighborhood schools are often the anchors of their communities, a steady presence that help cement the bonds for people and their social, economic, and political activities. Without viable school programs and resources to support progressive community development, far too many urban youth will continue to struggle to achieve effective results. Essentially, schools are community resources that dictate the pulse and vibrancy of a neighborhood. Schools leverage and stabilize communities, which creates a cultural identity and legacy for a people. If policyholders and business leaders invested in communities the way they continue to develop charter and contract schools, it would make a tremendous amount of difference for neighborhoods. Once again, communities would become proud of the schools within their neighborhood. Rarely have the American society invested in urban areas similar to how they fund the military, banks, and private offshore corporations. It is no coincidence communities with a solid tax base and effective resources display thriving schools in America. Recent reports and data from Research for Action suggest that school closings create education desserts in areas of the city with the highest concentration of minority and low-income residents (Hing 2013).

Schools are often the last surviving institution left in a neighborhood. The voracity to which schools are being changed and removed from the pages of Chicago's south and west side of the city makes one question how many traditional public schools will actually stay put in black and brown communities. With the current precedence of more than fifty-plus school closures, it is probably for certain there will exist very few public schools in major urban cities. Any remaining schools will function as a magnet or special enrollment school achieving high assessment marks, limited social challenges, and a pre-enrolled academically prepared student body.

During Western expansion, otherwise known as Manifest Destiny, it became readily apparent that specific groups had to become displaced to develop territories. Railroads and meatpacking industries were the new capital staple for capitalists seeking to grow their businesses. This sadly forced Native American indigenous groups to resettle to different parts of the nation, especially Oklahoma (Gwynne 2011). At first, the government, alongside policyholders and investors, promised Native Americans prosperity and stability if they compromised to relocate and develop farmland oasis in deserted western territories. Besides attempting to farm and cultivate land, something they had no experience or skills to perform, they had to compromise their culture and former homes to resettle in Western towns. Many indigenous cultures resisted this compromise and fought the advancement of Western expansion. Despite their gallant attempts, agreements, and concessions, industrial entrepreneurs and commercial prospectors to rebuild the West displaced Native populations (Gwynne 2011).

History is replete with examples of how Native Americans were forced to settle on reservations, abandon and sacrifice their traditions by submitting to cultural hegemony, and surrender their former lands to "progress." Notwithstanding, the railroad turned out to be a powerful symbol of an end of Native Americans' legacy in the West.

So is the case for Charter schools in urban America, which represent a private expansion and takeover of public education. Many are coerced to flee the city because they are priced out from gentrification, urban decay, and violence. In addition, inconsistent school policies and closures, along with ethno-demographic shifts influence minorities to venture elsewhere to find a positive middle ground for their families. Those families that could afford to leave migrated from the city some time ago. As recent reports suggest, Chicago's black middle class has lost more than 17 percent of its population in the last few years, which translates to more than two hundred thousand blacks having migrated from the city (Swendlow 2014; Lipman 2011).

Spiking foreclosure rates in South Side and West Side neighborhoods increased the already high number of vacant and abandoned homes, making those areas less popular with middle-income blacks (Swendlow 2014). Not to mention the fact high crime and increasing poverty rates have helped persuade blacks to move to higher ground with the pursuing flood of urban social challenges (e.g., gun violence, murder rates, closing schools, failing schools). To access quality, magnet, and high-achieving select enrollment schools deeply depends on the number of enrollment slots available, a 90 percent percentile student assessment score in the areas of math, reading, and English, and nearly straight As on a student report card (Kamp 2010). How many students are able to produce such results is contingent on their academic skills and testing abilities; moreover, their educational profile, ethnic background, and family status determines entry into a high-performing school. Just having these admirable attributes does not mean a student will become accepted into one of these schools. In fact, there is about a 30 percent chance a student meeting the aforementioned requirements will obtain entry into a select enrollment school (Kamp 2010).

School closures have accelerated throughout America's urban terrain. Similar to industrialist and commercialist displacing Native Americans from their lands to support capitalist expansion, schools represent the end of an era gone by to benefit private development. Throughout the country mass urban schools closures are happening because the public is told districts lack money, schools are failing students, or enrollment is low. Charter schools have a lot to say about why districts lack money, because in many instances, they are competing for tax dollars and students to spur their educational models. Charter schools account for more than 30 percent of traditional public students (Ravitch 2014). It is no wonder why public schools are struggling to keep their doors open due to low enrollment, because a lot of their students have left to attend charter schools. Mary Filardo with Twenty-First Century School Fund argues charter schools have fueled declining enrollment in many urban public schools by filling up their own classrooms (Strauss 2012).

Closing schools does not save money yet costs taxpayers more in the end to channel resources, students, and faculty to new facilities. Originally it was believed school closures would result in less expenditure as a way to consolidate resources and cut salaries. Unfortunately, this has become a toxic option for many districts journeying down this road because school boards still have to provide maintenance, security, resources, transportation, and personnel training to accommodate new students. Changes cost money and may not often translate or mean new quality results. The bottom line from Filardo's perspective is that no matter what anyone says, keeping kids in school means you will have to pay to help them achieve. Regardless of the intent of charter schools managing their sites at a lesser cost than traditional schools, it has not worked out too well for them in recent years. Initially, it was alleged that charter schools would excel at a cheaper tax rate. Today, they are begging districts and policyholders to increase per-pupil expenditure cost to better compete with traditional public school budgets.

Current school data projections about charter-school performances versus public school achievement actually do not vary by much. Actually, some public schools continue to outperform charter schools despite the amount of expenditure, support, and resources forward to these arrangements. Research from Stanford University further showed that while charter schools in Philadelphia and Chicago appeared to have a slight edge of performance over some of the public schools, more than half were underperforming against their predecessors (Goldstein 2013). Most of the displaced student bodies from school closures will not academically benefit attending new educational facilities. Ironically, students and parents are attending similar school arrangements they recently fled.

It further appears the restructuring of school communities and neighborhoods is not a new construct. Urban renewal and school revitalization plans appeared in the late 1950s and '60s with the *Brown v. Board of Education* decision. When specific communities were forced to integrate their schools, a mass exodus of white populations occurred resulting in the development of new schools and neighborhoods. To more effectively accommodate white populations, resources were redistributed from recent integrated domains to homogenized school districts with a higher tax base (Kozol 2006). This led to a considerable amount of unified schools to deteriorate in terms of infrastructure and capital improvement as financial assets were rerouted to neighboring white districts. The effects were disastrous for many merging schools as skilled teachers fled, the ethnography of communities shifted, and a stable flow of tax dollars evaporated. This not only helped cripple the *Brown v. Board*'s decision to tear down school segregation, it ruined many cities' plans to invest in school zones. Such long-term disinvestment led to poor schools and communities. Decades later, it is no wonder public schools functioning in these neighborhoods struggle to maintain their solvency. Rather than invest in these schools deemed blighted, the course of action has been to turn them over to private investors as a way to develop new assets, capital, and strategies to educate minority students. More importantly, the ultimate plan is to take a wrecking ball to many of these school communities using charter schools to reform the system.

Displacement

During the height of immigration to the states in the late nineteenth century, skilled and unskilled labor was employed within factories at a cheap rate. Owners and private investors would minimally pay workers while at the same time not providing them proper compensation such as, medical compensation and health benefits. If a worker was injured on a job, scabs or another worker in need of employment easily replaced them. Factory bosses and capitalist took advantage of their employees, even going so far as to hire children to support the manufacturing of raw materials and commodities. Essentially, labor was outsourced from Europe at the end of the Civil War to not only replace white populations decimated from the war but to lock out the black skilled labor class that established the nation's burgeoning economy (Bennett 1993).

Eventually, immigrant whites, many of who recently fled from English colonized territory, formed unions to develop employment protections against greedy, exploitative owners (Ignatiev 2008). Major resistance from owners ensued, which led to employment strikes, sabotage of worksites, production slowdowns, and violence. Quite a number of fatalities occurred as workers fought owners and police over unfair employment practices. What unions helped to provide to places of employment is irrefutable. From health benefits and humane working hours to improved wages and labor clauses, unions helped establish civil working environments for Americans.

How quickly we forget when today it is argued, by some circles of society, that unions are no longer necessary. In 1980, President Ronald Regan foiled an air traffic control strike by firing all unionized employees. At one point, the strikes threatened to shut down many airports across the nation. Instead, the union no longer existed, and the federal government could privately contract employees to work at the airport. Employees working in this industry received a major cut in pay, increased hours, and few benefits to brag about under the new contract. What Regan did was to simply turn back the clock on years of labor improvement.

The new sociopolitical term that best-defined Regan's action is *regimento*, which essentially meant a rearticulating of the existing social order (Omi and Winat 1994). The term originates from French enslavers and colonizers of the sixteenth century that methodically reengineered the cultural practices of Africans. Similar to French enslavers of yesteryear, owners of production have reformatted labor to better serve the altar of Adam Smith's capitalist deity. Throughout the country almost every labor pool has been converted to a worker-right or same-day employee status, which means absolutely no protection from unfair labor practices, limited growth earnings, and intensive site restrictions and monitoring. More importantly, a person could be fired without substantiated logic. It just so happens today's public schools are undergoing this same paradigm shift, an umbrella of Ronald Regan's regimento practice, to end the unionized practice of teachers. This not only protects the interest of private managers of education, it makes educators expendable assets of school improvement. From 2004 to 2012, with the emergence of No Child Left Behind (NCLB) and Race to the Top federal school legislative policies, approximately three hundred thousand public school teachers have been let go of their jobs since the emergence of charter schools (Ravitch 2014).

Couple this with the fact that from 2008 to 2012 the average state has lost anywhere from 16,677.9 public teaching positions and laid off 6,096.7 people, accounting for 35 percent of employment cuts since 2008 (Watkins 2011). Newly hired charter schoolteachers fresh out of college enter the profession, similar to the scabs (people willing to break picket lines to work in place of striking employees) of the nineteenth century, unaware of the intended treatment headed their direction. According to a Vanderbilt Peabody Study in 2008, Twenty –five percent of charter schoolteachers turned over during the 2003-2004 year, compared to 14 percent of traditional public school teachers. Fourteen percent of charter school teachers left the profession outright, and 11 percent moved to a different school, while 7 percent of traditional public schoolteachers left the profession and 7 percent relocated to another school in the district (Stult and Smith 2009).

Without unions or protection from their employers, a revolving door surfaces within the profession that works to destroy the moral and collegial investment educators make toward students. Communities and learners suffer the most from this arrangement because they do not receive long-term commitments from practitioners skilled to work within their environments to make quality improvements. The report furthers suggest a charter schoolteacher has a 76 percent greater chance of moving schools versus a traditional public school educator (Stult and Smith, 2009). To effectively turn around a school, it takes on average five or six years with an effective staff and support personnel (Watkins 2011). If all indication is clear, private managers and policyholders of current school reform suggest it should take a minimum of two to three years to improve the assessment and academic abilities of learners. This poses a real challenge when contemplating years of neglect, limited resources, and slashed budgets some schools have undergone. The amount of difficulty it takes to transform a school in two to three years seems a bit absurd and purposefully deliberates the closure of facilities falling short to make a miracle happen. Even when schools make annual incremental gains, it is clearly not enough for policyholders because they still close their doors deeming their attempts futile.

Recent stories in Chicago indicate several schools were barely saved or taken off the chopping block due to incredible gains made by schools within the last few years (McInerney 2013). More disturbing, 88 percent of school closures occur in black and brown communities across the nation, usually displacing hundreds of black and brown educators (Ravitch 2010). Upon being terminated from a school labeled failing, it is extremely hard for educators to find employment in newly opened or restructured schools. As a result, many minority teachers encounter tremendous employment obstacles attempting to reassert themselves into a system declaring them ineffective. The number of black educators out of work is startling. As recent labor report indicates, "Fifty-five percent of teachers who lost their jobs this past year are people of color, 45 percent of which are Black teachers" (Wiltz 2015). In Chicago, the number of black educators has dropped from 42 percent in the year 2006 to 21.5 percent in 2012 (McInerney 2013).

With a disproportionate amount of black educators being forced from the system in an already deeply segregated and divided school structure, many students of color are often left with inexperienced white teachers who stay around on average two years before declaring they've had enough. When newly opened charter schools declare they cannot find any quality black teaching candidates in their application pool, what they are really saying is: "We cannot hire recently fired teachers who happen to be black from failing schools." Not surprising, the average new charter school located in urban communities has a black employment population of 11.6 percent compared to 85.3 percent of white teachers (Catalyst Chicago 2014). Of course, some charter schools may fare higher in terms of black employment trends, yet a cruel fact remains that there exists a considerable number of black educators out of work. Job disparities have become so great within education, black children are lucky to discover a teacher of color reflecting, identifying, and relating to their cultural past. Usually if blacks are employed in these charter schools, they compose 42 percent of the instructional support staff, 65 percent of custodial services, and 72 percent of cafeteria workers (Catalyst 2010). This becomes even more disturbing because it suggests blacks cannot teach, but they sure as hell know how to serve. What message is further being sent to children of color when they discover that all the black educators are seated in the back of the cafeteria? In some sort of strange way, Reagan's regimento has forwarded education into a new Jim Crow practice and policy of hiring people of color, which translates into black people barely having a job in education.

Fixing this perplexing challenge will truly take a certain amount of effort, courage, and sacrifice similar to the battles waged from unionized immigrants in the nineteenth century. Untold are the number of professionals marching and fighting for productive non-co-opted school change as these issues are being discussed. It is also clear black educators have to reinvent their practice and efforts to teach their youth. No longer can they continue to rely on a Jim Crow system of urban education and private development to dictate teaching and learning in their communities. To once again empower themselves and assert their knowledge and skills to practice a liberating pedagogy to their children, the concept of freedom schools must emerge or surface to counter white hegemonic schooling practices and policies.

PART V

How Freedom Schools Help Educators Navigate School Reform

Still Waters

During the mid-1920s and '30s African American activist and educators begin to seek new school reform efforts to better educate their children. Since African American schools were already sophistically segregated and direly underfunded, many crusaders believed it was essential to establish schools that served the best interest of their children. Activist such as Marcus Garvey, Elijah Muhammad, and Mary McCleod Bethune developed independent and cultural-based institutions to counter inept school practices. Initially created to train African Americans to acquire work in the vocational trades similar to Booker T. Washington's Tuskegee model, they eventually saw the need to also intellectually train and prepare their scholars to become the defenders and practitioners of the race. Educators, lawyers, physicians, and engineers would soon emerge from these institutions grounded in the theory of cultural and civil liberation.

Educational liberators like Marcus Mosaic Garvey developed schools within his Pan-African movement to train and equip blacks to manage and control their own economic, political, and social affairs. Garvey understood that African Americans' roles in traditional schools was underserved and marginalized. As a best practice to do away with this type of educational tutelage, Garvey instituted pre-kindergarten and elementary school arrangements that taught African Americans the basic skills of arithmetic, science, and language arts while instilling within them their own cultural history (Cronon and Franklin 1960). Many participants within Garvey's organization had recently fled southern jurisdictions and regions possessing little more than a third- or fourth-grade education. The result of sharecropping and debt peonage systems coerced African Americans to the agrarian fields versus schooling. To help parents and their families financially survive harsh economic times, many children had to work in the fields to harvest crops versus being schooled on the ABCs. When African Americans were able to emerge from these arrangements, they sought new opportunities for their families and children.

Garvey's movement came into its own post-World War I. African American veterans returning from the war, along with urban families living in segregated cities, sought a new direction for their future. Garvey's parades, cultural attire, and sheer vocal charisma appealed to their senses, informing them they held a true place in this world.

Despite some African American leaders finding Garvey's message flawed and exaggerated, his movement continued to attract individuals wanting to produce their own institutions. Garvey established the first black nurses association or union, several elementary and high schools, a health care facility, daycare centers, and a direct-relief agency. The Black Star Line, ships purchased to establish trade routes and financial transactions between Europe, Asia, and Africa, were created to economically invest and empower African American communities. Through the Black Star Line, black businesses could exchange their products and resources on a global scale, no longer depending on just the African American community for financial survival (Garvey 2013).

Sadly, these powerful institutions Garvey established deflated as a result of economic scandal and poor fiscal management. It also did not help that the FBI set up counterintelligence operatives to sabotage the successes and outcomes of Garvey's movement (Cronon and Franklin 1960). However, Garvey's school arrangement was unique and powerful. He built his model from his mentor and role model, Booker T. Washington, believing it would provide blacks with the sort of skills necessary to craft their own institutions.

Garvey's aims were clear:

- nationalize African Americans to develop their own independent economic base;
- expand black businesses to network and operate beyond the borders of white America;
- establish and insulate a work force that trains and prepares blacks to manage businesses; and
- guide, instruct, and prepare the youth to acquire educational and economic skills to support their own communities.

Garvey's thinking was resolute and clear, which helped blacks navigate the waters of white supremacy and economic oppression. Garvey's movement also served as a way to defend African Americans from public policies that restricted their successful social transition and mobility. Despite Garvey's inability to sustain the powerful notion of financial independence and sovereignty for African Americans, he left a model or blueprint for them to pursue. One such example was his freedom schools, which imparted a proficient and competent amount of literacy and math development for African American youth. It also increased students' abilities to obtain a high degree of efficacy to promote their independent thinking to create institutions that serviced the needs of their community.

Similar to Garvey's initiatives, Elijah Muhammad established the Sister Claire Muhammad Schools, named after his wife, to counter white supremacy and social policies of the north and south. Like Garvey, Muhammad built his schools to teach his followers to become economically independent of the white people. His school model was established to accomplish several important principles:

- train and prepare African Americans to develop their own businesses;
- morally train and equip African Americans to abide by a strict ethnical code of self-help, discipline, and behavioral practices to counter hegemony;
- instill a high degree of cultural pride and awareness to competently develop independent thinking; and
- acquire skills that serviced the needs of the community (Evanzz 2011).

A former follower of Garvey himself, Muhammad picked up where Garvey had left off to successfully transition African Americans (Latif, N and Latif, S 1994). Initially, Muhammad had a very small following of four hundred. His religious thinking and spiritual perspectives were detached and unique from the traditional Protestant practices of African American Christians. Yet his message of social, political, and economic reform appealed to followers that believed in his notion of self-reliance and independence. Muhammad's message soon expanded and circulated upon recruiting his greatest pupil, Malcolm X (Marble 2010).

Malcolm himself, schooled to the philosophies of Garvey by his parents, who were followers of his message, believed African Americans should manage their own institutions to equip their people. Unfortunately, Malcolm in his youth became wayward or delinquent on his journey. From his father's murder from apparent Klan activity to his mother's nervous breakdown, Malcolm, similar to so many African American youth today, became detached, confused, and an embittered renegade as a result of his family desolation. Malcolm's illicit behavior eventually landed him in prison for theft and embezzlement of stolen property for eight years.

It was in prison where Malcolm learned of the teachings of Muhammad from his brother, Reginald. At first, Malcolm believed Muhammad's message could be used as a sort of hustle or con to reduce his prison sentence. However, as Malcolm began to study Muhammad's teachings, they soon resonated the same message he had learned from his parents. Malcolm was hooked, and Muhammad's teaching transformed his character and moral self. As a follower of Muhammad, Malcolm became his greatest ally and pupil, recruiting and helping establish more spiritual centers to support members. Eventually, Malcolm helped publish Muhammad's first major newspaper, which also helped spread his leader's message.

Upon increasing numbers within Muhammad's organization, more members needed schools for their children to attend. The Sister Claire Muhammad School expanded and academically prepared many African American youth in major cities from the late-1950s through the '70s (Evanzz 2013). The recruitment of Malcolm's efforts helped establish Sister Claire Muhammad as a major educational institution in the African American community. Parents and families who were not necessarily followers of Muhammad recognized the considerable attributes and program's initiatives offered to students. A great many parents began snatching their children from failing public schools to enroll them into Muhammad's schools. Chicago, Detroit, New York, and Philadelphia had the largest enrollment of students attending Sister Claire Muhammad schools. The message was clear for families and students attending the school:

- African Americans must develop and create their own institutions independent of the white power structure to financially survive;
- African Americans must become highly skilled scholars invested in the fields of science and math to advance technology, medicine, and nutrition;

- African Americans should master language arts and history to counter hegemony while promoting their own publishing companies such as newspapers, printing presses, and electronic media to enlighten and inform their people; and
- African Americans must develop businesses that support and sustain their community.

It is no coincidence that students graduating from a Sister Claire Muhammad school found success in major fields such as science, medicine, and education (Evanzz 2013). Despite the school not receiving any sort of government support or funding, participants at the school paid reduced tuition rates along with receiving financial assistance from similar religious organizations, members, and donors. Similar to Garvey, a blueprint had been established for African Americans to follow if they ever want to escape elite venture capitalists' privatized educational plans for their children.

Like Garvey, Muhammad's movement saw a decline as once again government provocateurs established disharmony and dissension among the rank and file of the organization. Eventually, Malcolm X and Muhammad fell on bad terms, which caused Malcolm to leave the organization. Membership in Muhammad's organization suffered as a result of Malcolm's departure. Malcolm was regrettably assassinated in 1965 while working to establish his own structure. Muhammad in due course passed away in 1975, leaving the organization to his son and family members. This resulted in the organization having another major split, which led to restructuring in 1978 by Louis Farrakhan.

Today, Muhammad's organization continues to expound the teaching and message of its former leader, but sadly it is nowhere near what it was in the past. The Sister Claire Muhammad School was renamed to Muhammad University of Islam. Membership has dwindled to little more than fifty thousand followers, once having peaked at four hundred thousand followers in 1963 (Evanzz 2013). Although the school continues to have tremendous success with students, enrollment remains low, hurting the school's ability to financially resource school programs and projects. However, the model remains a powerful symbol of what kinds of schools should become developed to service the needs of African American children.

Mary McLeod Bethune, another amazing pioneer of education, understood at a young age the importance of ascertaining important skills and information to compete in the economy. Raised as a sharecropper's daughter, as the fifteenth child out of seventeen, she was instilled with the importance of an education from her parents. Several people took an active interest in her education, and she attended school in South Carolina. While most African American children were forced to leave school to help their parents in the field, Bethune was able to stay put to learn the basics of education.

Learn she did, as Bethune became a model student and dedicated learner of her studies. Eventually, the same people who saw her incredible knack for education at school, church members, educators, missionaries, donors, and homesteaders believed she could prosper in college (Greenfield and Pickney 1994). Bethune went on to attend Scotia Seminary for four years and from there became an educator at Haines Normal and Industrial Institute at Augusta, Georgia. These institutions were missionary schools performing various types of social work around the world, most notably in Africa. Although Bethune desired to teach in Africa, she was denied this opportunity by her colleagues, believing she was more needed at home versus abroad.

Bethune then set her sights on opening her very own school in Daytona, Florida. Like Booker T. Washington with his Tuskegee Institute, Bethune discovered a small property near abandoned territory that could be utilized to build a school. Once again, the same individuals who financed her education also supported her efforts in Daytona, Florida. Bethune's school initially serviced girls, six to start, training them in literacy and industrial education. Similar to Muhammad, Bethune saw a need to stress the importance of spiritual values to morally mold and equip African American youth to function in society. Training in industry not only stressed seamstress, textile manufacturing, and trade development, but her school also taught home economics, etiquette, and self-sufficiency. As her school expanded, she required more financial assistance to manage her affairs. This support came from none other than Booker T. Washington and supporters of his, believing Bethune's school was a critical necessity to prepare African American females for participation in the economy. Bethune also believed educating females was important because having productive women in the community would advance the race. Women were not only important cultural assets and pioneers for families, they managed the domestic affairs of the household. Their abilities and skills would strengthen the African American family and advance the intellectual and emotional needs of children.

Bethune's school became a true representation of an independent freedom school. Her success and recognition grew, and she eventually became a spokesperson for women rights, civil rights, and educational discourse. The first lady Eleanor Roosevelt later embraced her political observations and perspectives. Essentially, this provided Bethune with a national platform, expanding her ideas and concepts about education.

Bethune-Cookman University remains today as an important institutional pillar teaching African American females and males alike. There is no telling how many success stories Bethune accomplished, beginning a very small schoolhouse in Daytona, Florida. However, it speaks volumes as to what can be accomplished by African Americans seeking new alternatives to private-venture school reforms.

Freedom Schools

The term "freedom school" initially took it roots from the canopies of chattel slavery, where children were taught basic literacy and math skills from the loins of a slave master's wife, a freedman visiting the plantation, or a servant learning how to read (Douglass 1995). Under the fledgling guard and whip of a master's disregard, enslaved Africans were encouraged to not learn how to read, write, and perform mathematics because they would surely outflank and intellectually challenge their oppressor. It was also taught by mainstream white society that African Americans were genetically inept to become educated; therefore, it was useless to teach them. Countless African Americans and former enslaved Africans disproved this "retarded" notion by not only mastering the basic skills of education but by launching their own entrepreneurial, intellectual, and social institutions.

The next phase of freedom schools surfaced from abolitionists within northern territories that constructed educational centers to teach literacy skills to African Americans. Children and adults flocked to these schools many of which were also supported by church organizations equipping their religious sites with classrooms to support African Americans' educational needs (Anderson 1988). A great number of children benefited from these arrangements as they learned important spiritual values and intellectual ideas. Ultimately, churches became the main resource of helping educate children of color denied this very same exercise in society.

The emergence of freedom schools also took root in the south after the Civil War. Carpetbaggers, former abolitionists, government officials, and recently freed people took the initiative to develop academies servicing the intellectual needs of African Americans. Freedmen schools, as they were referred, set out to teach literacy and mathematics as a way to counter years of educational oppression from chattel slavery. Millions of African Americans participated in these schools as teachers, principals, students, donors, and advocates academically enriched and trained the race for advancement (Bennett 1993). For them, education served as a cornerstone and pathway to create more social and economic opportunities. Unfortunately, the downturn of this schooling practice submerged as the Restoration Act of 1877 was legislated, renewing a denial of African Americans educational opportunities in the south. In addition, scandal and economic pillaging from government officials in 1873 deeply underfunded any attempts to sufficiently finance and resource freedmen schools (Anderson 1988). Regardless of the schools success rates and attempts to educate recently freed African Americans, policyholders believed they had done enough to deliver former President Lincoln's Reconstruction acts.

Originally starting out as a way to help register African Americans to vote while teaching them political literacy, freedom schools once again emerged during the mid-1960s in the South by Civil Rights activist seeking to reform Jim Crow laws. A number of white and African American activists flooded the south, similar to carpetbaggers during the Reconstruction Era, to alter racial oppression and social deformity. White terrorists and southern policyholders saw these activists as a threat to their way of life; consequently, they worked to destroy the freedom schools.

Besides teaching constitutional rights and voting initiatives, Civil Rights workers also taught academic courses such as reading, writing, and math skills to enhance children's educational concepts. Quite a number of African American adults and children were illiterate, particularly in Mississippi, where Jim Crow laws had successfully suppressed any attempts to receive a quality education. Segregated schools in the south were drastically underfunded, resources were limited, and books, paper, and writing utensils were nonexistent. Civil Rights activist brought supplies and ample reading materials to support the educational needs of children. In addition, many children had to attend the field versus schooling to support their parents and families' agrarian lifestyle (McAdam 1990).

Consequently, Civil Rights workers had to employ an effective schedule or time of day to intellectually interact and engage their students. A protocol of support and trust emerged between the workers and populations, which helped to grow the movement. Freedom schools were an effective way to service students while recruiting registered voters. Of course this did not rest well with the southern power structure, which led to unbridled attacks, murders, and sabotage of the workers' affairs. The most notable case occurred in 1964 with the murders of James Chaney, Andrew Goodman, and Michael Schwerner by members of the Ku Klux Clan. Their murders were nationally and internationally recognized as intolerable proving federal intervention was necessary to stop racist activity (McAdam 1990).

Despite these terrorist attempts, the workers continued their zeal and passion to intellectually liberate and register African American voters to shift power in the south. Unopposed to the threats, beatings, bombings, and murders, white and African American citizens pushed forth the concept of freedom schooling. Today, more than ever, Civil Rights workers of the past serve as a great inspiration of what needs to occur to counter current school reform mandates from private venture capitalist. Their struggle, spirit, energy, and sheer attempts to stand in the face of opposition bent to destroy their efforts speaks volumes as to why freedom schools are more necessary than ever in today's urban America.

Than came "power to the people," a radical phrase expressed by members of the Black Panther Party seeking liberation from the shackles of white oppression in a number of ways. Contrary to arming followers with a black tam, leather jacket, and assault rifle, members of the Black Panther Party also set up freedom schools in major cities to culturally educate and enlighten community members. Leaders of the movement, Hewey P. Newton and Bobby Seal, were highly educated and industrious activist from Oakland, California, successfully spreading their organizations into other cities such as Chicago, New York, Philadelphia, and LA. Advocates for self-empowerment and socialist reform, the party extolled the principles of Malcolm X, Elijah Muhammad, and Marcus Garvey. Not only did they believe the African American community needed to protect and defend itself from cultural hegemony, they believed the people should restore or rebuild the framework of existing structures through a ten-point plan.

Besides exposing cultural rhetoric and social reform about the evils of capitalist development, the Black Panther Party also equipped community members with sophisticated knowledge and information. Literacy was a major part of the movement, from reading Mao Zedong's *Red Book of Gorilla Warfare* to Karl Marx's *Communist Manifesto*. Enacting and applying critical literacy assisted the community's effort to improve neighborhoods plagued by crime, drug abuse, gang activity, poverty, and murder (Bloom and Martin 2013).

The Black Panther Party really enveloped steam in the late 1960s after the murder of Dr. Martin Luther King Jr. His death spoke volumes about why the party believed it was dire to enact a resistance movement to counter racism. To assist their efforts, the party established freedom schools, which included a free breakfast program, teaching African American children the importance of nutrition and civic-minded principles. Cultural history and lessons were shared to children while the basic three Rs were applied to empower their interest and focus to achieve a quality education. The party also created health clinics, daycare centers, businesses, and grocery stores to service the community. Similar to Garvey and contrary to skeptics, the Panthers believed their service to the community improved the everyday affairs, behavior, and perspectives of people.

The party suffered a tremendous blow when in 1969, FBI leader J. Edgar Hoover declared the Panthers "Public Enemy Number One" (Bloom and Martin 2013). Radical tendencies such as establishing allegiance with organized gangs in an effort to support the renewal of the community, coupled with various shootouts with local police departments, did not help matters. The murders of Fred Hampton, Bunchy Carter, Bobby Hutton, and Mark Clark, who were well known national Panther Party leaders and members, from police raids and clandestine provocateur activity sealed the Panthers' fate as local, state, and federal agencies zeroed in to destroy the organization. Lost in this discussion was the tremendous efforts and assistance the Panther Party leveraged to the community. From medically treating sickle cell anemia, teaching literacy courses, holding entrepreneurial classes, developing community organizational strategies, and offering crisis counseling, the Party showered many resourceful services to people. In addition, the free breakfast and lunch programs, busing, medical check ups, and clothing distribution emphatically represented the achievements of their freedom school approach. Today, many schools have adopted the Panthers' breakfast and lunch programs along with health checkups to service school communities. The Panthers left a tremendous legacy of how effective freedom schools can become utilized to support the interest of children and adults. What is even clearer, school reform and development must come from the bowels of the people.

A New Endeavor

My new teaching assignment brought a new sense of purpose and zeal working with a diverse student population. Again, the school was one of a few public-performing options made available to artistic learners. On average, a performing arts high school costs anywhere from $30,000 to $40,000 a year. The establishment of the school brought a certain amount of recognition and admiration from local officials, educators, and policyholders. Far too many public schools extinguished their budgets to manage funding to maintain academic programs, which meant art programs and special instructional classes were cut from many schools. In fact, some schools were forced to add a longer day without any extracurricular activities to support students' mental focus and maintenance in the classrooms. Instead, students were required to take an additional math and reading class rather than having a music, graphic design, dancing, or theater course. Sadly, some schools had to close down their sport programs just to keep teachers on the payroll. Most recently in Chicago, more than seventeen hundred specialty teachers were laid off, accounting for 19 percent of the workforce (Catalyst Chicago 2015). This occurred despite fifty school shutdowns, the largest educational closures recorded, which registered about three thousand more educators let go of their positions (Catalyst Chicago 2014).

Let's just say having employment in Chicago is a blessing and a curse. It is a blessing to work in a creative arts school where learners are excited to acquire pre-professional training and strong academic preparation. Why a curse? The climate and culture of education has created a toxic environment for teachers because there exists so much pressure to perform. When an instructor does not satisfy summative assessment expectations, instructional delivery standards, or an ideal management of their classes they are immediately terminated with little recourse. Pressure yields certain results and can either help a person produce quality results or shrink them into obscurity (Ravitch 2010).

A study was conducted at Stanford University in the late 1980s specifically targeting female math performances. The hypothesis of the study asserted white female learners perform poorly in mathematics because traditional instructional practices and approaches are tailored to support males (Lubiano 1998). The study worked from the premise that girls taking math had fewer opportunities to solve a difficult task, interact with a teacher, facilitate discussions, or be recognized as an ideal math student in a classroom. The study further noted that more males attended math degreed programs versus females; hence, there exists a tremendous labor shortage of women engineers, technology experts, and applied mathematical professionals.

During the study, a control and experimental group consigned females into separate learning categories. All of the subjects were straight-A students in high school. The experimental group was placed under more pressure, ridiculed for not answering questions, timed to complete assignments, held under close scrutiny, and made to feel insecure about their level of competency. Such a police approach directed toward these learners led to a negative performance.

The girls in the experimental group performed poorly and begged to drop out of the program. However, the control group did not undergo any restricted time or intentional instructional distractions to prohibit their performance. In fact, the girls outperformed males within the same mathematical program when permitted intellectual autonomy and management of their performance space. They also were encouraged and praised for attempting to solve challenging tasks versus ridiculed for failing to do so. This study is applicable for the teaching profession because so many educators are enduring excessive amounts of duress from their working arenas; consequently, their level of performance and focus toward developing creative instructional tasks has diminished. Instead teachers are developing lessons tailored specifically to state assessments, which by the way is being encouraged by administrators and business-managed school leaders to obtain specific results. The joy of educating children has withered in recent years for educators as more schools push for success on high stake tests.

Finding myself within this new teaching construct made me feel more tension versus working within the administrative setting. Despite this, I set my sights on working with students by building connections, relating content and subject information to their experiences, differentiating instructional materials, applying experiential and facilitative classroom methods, and establishing effective community partnerships with colleagues, administrators, and parents. Not to mention it took immense time to write a curriculum for world studies, grade papers, develop assessments, monitor grades, and check in with students, parents, and advisory teachers. It became especially cumbersome ensuring the success of special-needs students to abide by their learning accommodations and modifications. Overall, I spent countless hours working to prepare instructional plans to manage the success of students.

To say a teacher spends roughly six hours within their teaching day is ludicrous and insulting. The average effective teacher must spend a minimum of eight-and-a-half to ten hours daily to achieve quality results in their classroom (Wong 2009). What I especially enjoyed working with these learners was the amount of creativity and enthusiasm they showed toward discovering new concepts, information, and materials. I found myself utilizing college materials, particularly for advanced students who excelled at everything I intellectually threw at them. This sort of challenge and inquiry was completely new for me, which made me want to work even harder to advance students.

At the end of the school year, I was exhausted teaching 150 students, each one having his or her own personality, needs, and expectations.

The school year was especially rewarding because I was able to work with motivated special-needs learners. They were engaged, enthused, and eager to learn the skills and concepts in the classroom. In particular, the students really demonstrated their talents when exposed to creative and diverse instructional practices. This is where applying an art-integrated teaching approach became a best-practice method to support their learning levels. The materials or content seem to radically engage their ability to complete tasks while improving their literacy skills. From using different techniques to apply timed-reading exercises, text structure supports, reciprocal teaching, learning logs, inquiry research, visual-arts project-based assessments, and academic notebooks, I found myself immersed in the idea of abiding by these strategies to help all learners irrespective of their skill-sets or learning maturity.

It helped that I acquired special education credentials fours years earlier when teaching at my previous high school. I believed the methods and comprehensive strategies in special education could be universally applied to support struggling students. This experience also promoted my thirst to teach this population of learners, which I believed could benefit from my applied approaches versus abiding by new instructional standardized formats that I personally opposed and found difficulty adjusting my teaching style. In other words, I simply disapproved of directly teaching to the test for the purpose of improving language arts assessment scores. I fell in love and became too comfortable with traditional teaching approaches from the 1990s that taught instructors how to tailor creative educational methods to engage students. I strongly believed teaching special-needs learners could restore my enthusiasm and passion for education.

Toward the end of the school year I inquired about and applied for a special-needs position within the school when the school year closed. Now I was officially a special-education instructor with plenty of years of experience to support students.

As a new special education teacher, I discovered various strategies and techniques that could be used by teachers to empower students' literacy skills. To best support students' comprehension of reading materials or lessons, it was essential to make use of memory techniques, graphic organizers, brainstorming lessons, and relevant-inquiry scenario discussions to improve their literacy skills. Writing also was an important attribute and necessary asset to improve learners' literacy skills. Teaching them how to organize their writing, map out themes and details, develop expository structures, peer review and edit their papers, and creating topic questions to help them write became all necessary tools for them to increase their literacy skills. Once again, I found the joy of teaching students with diverse needs. Here I had my autonomy, limited scrutiny, personalized space to manage and facilitate instruction, an ability to design enrichment opportunities to support teachers and students, advance students' research abilities, and directly interact and counsel learners within a supportive arrangement. It also helped me to connect and support many of the extroverted and eccentric learners at the school, which made them unique and even more interesting working alongside them.

Teaching, for me, once again, became this powerful way to communicate with parents and students. Special education was an umbrella to support and sustain my efforts in education. More critical, was the intellectual transitions and skill improvements I could personally see occur working besides learners that traditionally struggled in education. For years, some of my students had been exposed to corrupt educational practices that hindered their growth and connection to school practices. A great deal of the learners simply lacked confidence to compete and succeed alongside other students to advance their abilities. Traditionally, special education learners encountered discriminatory practices and policies that stigmatized this population. With new laws and procedures via the Individuals with Disabilities Education Improvement Act, educators had to abide by a set of specific guidelines to ensure the support of learners. Services had to be resourced and classrooms integrated, no longer isolated and segregated, to support the transition of learners in public schools. Special education had come a long way from the first time I entered the profession. A lot of the strategies from special education were being used to support teachers struggling with challenging learners not necessarily deemed special needs. Another trend I saw unique in special education was as an instructor, you were not strictly evaluated on how well your students performed on state assessments.

Evaluations in Chicago public schools were based on Danielson's model of education:

- classroom preparation and rapport
- management and maintenance of students within the classroom
- communication with parents, students, and teachers
- maintenance of accurate usage of record keeping, written reports, and qualitative data
- collegial support and responsiveness to support students' academic needs

All of this was essential to make sure students received the right amount of support to help them successfully succeed in the classroom.

It also appeared from my perspective that special education was undergoing new changes within public schools, as though the service was being shuttered or inappropriately mishandled by bureaucrats. With more than fifty school closures in Chicago, quite a few specialized schools servicing elementary students were dismantled and reintegrated into existing sites. Some schools spent considerable fortunes to resource their institutions through the district support. Now the district could no longer afford their schools and had to close them down, thus rerouting children to neighboring locations. This seemed a very ineffective strategy and incredibly disturbing for many children already struggling with security and stability issues, particularly when these sites do not possess the infrastructure and resources to support special-needs learners. Many co-shared integrated classrooms will be overcrowded, intimidating, and managed poorly to accommodate these students (Ravitch 2010).

Having a structured and supportive environment is essential for special-needs learners to excel. According to a recent RAND study, Chicago approximately displaced 11 percent of its special-needs students into existing school models. Meaning the district lost or could not find schools transferring special needs students enrolled to receive educational services (Cannon 2013).

This same study also discussed how school closures had a disastrous effect on students' academic progress. It stated,

> One year after school closings, displaced special needs students who reenrolled in the weakest receiving schools

(those with test scores in the bottom quartile of all system schools) experienced an achievement loss of more than three months in reading and half a month in math. Meanwhile, students who reenrolled in the strongest receiving schools (those in the top quartile) experienced a loss of nearly one month in reading and more than two months in math. (Cannon, 2013)

The data suggests school reform is affecting children on multiple levels, especially students with special needs. Versus children gaining or maintaining consistent improvement transitioning to a different school, students' social-emotional needs are affected in a big way from educational closures. As a result, Chicago parents have recently filed a lawsuit to counter the district's closing of special needs schools. They assert the district is violating the Americans with Disabilities Act and Illinois Civil Rights Act.

Again, there are limited options available for educators deciding to work in this field. Even with the opportunity of working with special needs populations, a professional area once deemed secure has become laden with turmoil, dissension, and insecurity. It is already a field that requires a considerable amount of patience working with students experiencing anxiety disorders, autism, attention deficits, and other health impairments; not to mention academic challenges only increase the needs for teachers to constantly research and develop strategies to better support students. Now the district adds to this challenge by closing schools specifically targeted to support special-needs populations. My joy and love for this profession is truly diminishing thinking about the next educational tragedy. However, it is my hopes and prayers educators will survive this private-venture bureaucratic storm. This also speaks volumes as to why we require a fare share of freedom schools as an alternative choice to improve the morale of teachers, parents, and students residing in urban schools.

Exposure to Freedom Schools

Over the years I have made incredible observations of freedom schools serving the needs and interests of communities and families. From educating kindergarteners, seniors, and college students, these school models have helped thousands of learners successfully transition through life. Such schools have been very effective delivering a high quality education to students. The learning gap between white and black learners have narrowed because of these schools' ability to engage, academically prepare, and culturally empower students of color. Various professions and fields of study have benefited from graduates of freedom schools exposing their intellectual insights and theoretical understanding of social, political, and economic issues. Parents and communities benefited from these institutions because they provided alternative educational choices for parents escaping poor performing neighborhood schools. Freedom schools quest to reach the underserved and undesirables have reaped great benefits on society. Fewer students are incarcerated, and more have graduated from college due to freedom schools' facilitation and guidance of learning and social skills. Quite a number of students from these schools have careers as physicians, teachers, lawyers, civic leaders, policymakers, activists, and social workers. A number of them return to their former communities to support the neighborhoods

What makes these schools so effective is that they are community-based and centered to provide sustenance, care, and affirmation to black children, which sorely lacks in far too many educational institutions. It is no coincidence many children attending these schools have parents working in them (e.g., janitors, teachers, principals, instructional assistants, and community members).

Parent activism and volunteerism excels in these schools as parents make time to support programs, exploratory outings, fundraising events, mediation, and student patrol or escort services. Ultimately, freedom schools deliver where public, private, and charter institutions envision should happen to improve black achievement. It is also interesting to note community members and teachers manage freedom schools. Many teachers working in these schools left traditional learning sites to practice a liberating pedagogy. When public schools introduced the concept of local school councils, it came from the concept of freedom schools (Shujaa 1996). The only difference is that freedom schools are more authentic applying this practice to involve the community. Far too many local school councils are controlled and influenced by district school boards, policyholders, and mayoral managed systems to make any effective changes (Ravitch 2014). When parents are truly afforded a voice and decision making in the process of learning, it improves students' ability to excel and builds confidence in their character. As a result, a lot of graduating students leaving these schools return to volunteer, teach, and develop programs (Shujaa, 1994).

A Freedom School in A Hub City

A hub city is categorized as an urban space or terrain formerly developed that deteriorates from lack of economic investments (Dimitradis 2003). Hub cities usually rest as outliers away from traditional urban zones. Once developed by factories, industries, and a burgeoning job economy, capital investments retreated leaving abandon properties, businesses, and schools. Inner city environments similar to Compton, LA, Ferguson, Missouri, and Ford Heights, Illinois, are examples of hub cities. Some critics suggest that communities within cities exist as new hub cities because limited resources and capital investments are made to improve these areas.

Jacob Carruthers explored this same concept referring to these geographic spaces as inner city environments (Carruthers 1999). For him, these spaces were designed to relegate and contain African Americans and Latinos into distinct urban zones where their behaviors were micromanaged, restricted, and policed. Carruthers further asserts that such communities or spatial patterns are seen throughout the world, where elite populations typically retreated into their own terrain disadvantaging others by removing their resources from those populations. The inner city, from Carruthers' perspective, exists within urban spaces regardless to how wealthy or advanced centralized parts of the city emerge. Hence, a hub city similar to Carruthers' inner city domain exist as a forgotten or abandon geographic space denied similar advantages and supports unlike affluent or "acceptable areas" away from these urban zones (Lipman 2011). These spaces are segregated and apartheid-like, containing poor and working-class minorities. Crime ravages these communities with gang activity and gun violence existing at epidemic levels. Food and trauma hospital desserts flourish. Chicago under Daley's administration (1990–2010) advanced the notion of inner city hub dimensions over his twenty-year reign (Watkins 2011). As the economic gap grew wider between Chicago communities, more families, children, and schools were left behind to suffer receiving limited city resources and business investment to promote employment, healthy-food depositories, and youth enrichment programs.

With lack of investment and continued racial isolation, schools on Chicago's west and south sides further underperformed, causing middle-income families to migrate to better areas to raise their families. Similar to the 1960s and '70s black and "white flight" era consisting of middle income whites and blacks leaving the city relocating to suburban townships, those who remained could not afford to leave; consequently, they had to live in communities plagued by challenged behaviors, few low-paying jobs, and limited resources. Many families and their children gave up on the schools and their future. Neighborhoods such as Englewood, Roseland, Maple Park, and West Pullman on the south side remain in need of quality schools to support the redevelopment of their families and communities. It is no coincidence charter and contract schools petition their existence into these communities to directly provide alternative school choices for families.

However, as the data continues to demonstrate, charter schools' achievement scores measured by aptitude tests remain stagnate and not far removed from the performance of area public schools despite the vast amount of money, selected student bodies, and resources forward to them (Strauss 2014). It seemed these communities, in particular the Roseland neighborhood, desperately needed a freedom school to emerge.

I applied the following data collection methodology to triangulate my results observing two of the schools featured, Freedom Home International Academy (FHIA) and Village Leadership Academy (VLA):

- note taking
- unobtrusive observations
- historic research investigation
- unstructured interviewing

The theoretical formulations driving my research methodology are Gloria Ladson Billings' cultural responsive education (CRP) and Ali and Murphy's cultural value-driven (CVD) pedagogy, which suggests students better respond to instruction when the curriculum is relevant and connects to the core beliefs of their families, cultural heritage, and communities (Ladson-Billings 2005; Ali and Ryan 2013).

The first school I observed was Marcus Kline's Freedom Home International Academy located on the south side of Chicago in the Roseland community. Marcus Kline, better known as Baba Marcus, successfully manages this school. Prior to creating an independent school for students and parents, Marcus worked for years as a community activist and organizer to support urban development and educational enlightenment. At one time Marcus helped co-edit and finance a community paper known as *Frontline* publication, which effectively transmitted "eye browsing" global and domestic information to folks traditionally "turned off" by corporate news. Despite its controversy and introspective critique against capitalist elites and the hegemonic entities governing the world, it transmitted intriguing and responsive information to the community that invoked critical inquiry investigations. Marcus through his publication enhanced the discovery and discussion of "hidden knowledge" concealed from the masses, which readily increased people's intellectual capital countering the notion "ignorance is bliss."

While managing the magazine, Marcus eventually constructed an independent school inside his publication offices initially teaching intermediary grade levels. Parents in the community soon recognized the remarkable importance of the school and not only invested their time, energy, and money to enroll their children, but also recruited and marketed the school idea to other parents. This not only brought him closer with the community, but also spurred his desires to expand and make the model more available to the African American community. Students from the ages of four to twelve visited several countries in Africa, attended intellectual conferences, and participated in community volunteer efforts.

To further expand the construction of his institution, Marcus went to several communities to gain considerable support for his educational idea. Several educational activist and pioneers provided advice and financial support toward his school. Furthermore, this brought with it more parental involvement, networking, and political support that saw a critical need to create more effective quality schools in urban neighborhoods. Eventually Marcus was able to raise funds to expand his school.

Unlike the corporate, private-public arrangements seen through the eyes of charter and contract schools, Marcus's school was unique because he involved parents, educators, and activists to develop a curriculum that best met the needs of the community. As mentioned before, a curriculum should represent what a community really needs and wants for their children to learn. Unfortunately, too many new schools impose onto neighborhoods what they believe is "best" for them. Hence, there's not much difference with the way former colonial masters imposed their political, social, and economic will onto indigenous populations. Notwithstanding, Marcus's school promotes new synergy to develop quality education inclusive rather than dismissive. To continue the existence of his school framework and increase this resource to the community, Marcus was able to locate an abandon building further south of his existing school and purchase the property. The school officially now belonged to the community and was open for intellectual advancement rather than "business." Parents from the surrounding areas and other parts of the city flocked to the school, willing to invest in the institution's success. Marcus revised his school's name, calling it Freedom Home International Academy (FHIA), indicative of the historic narrative shaping African Americans' evolution away from traditional school plantation societies (Anderson 1988).

Marcus's freedom school results are magnificent. Students continue to improve their academic skills, gaining entry into the nation's best high schools and colleges. Student literacy and math skills continue to resonate high results from various national assessments and other summative evaluations (Chicago Public Schools 2014). Marcus's school curriculum is framed around an African-centered paradigm that teaches and incorporates the beliefs and practices of Dr. Molefi Asante and Dr. Jawanza Kunjufu. The school curriculum takes at its core the philosophical concept that education is an inward journey versus a rote-behavioral response system. Rather than memorizing information, formulas, and literacy strategies to pass standardized tests, students are intellectually nourished to connect to information and instruction to spur their cognitive development. Further framed around the concept of African-centered education, students are reinforced with the belief that knowledge already is a part of "who they are." Meaning humans were developed to desire learning as a connective part of their human experience to improve the world, instead of it being measured by one's material possessions or earnings. How well a person was behaved and intelligently responsive reflected their educational attainment.

Similar to Eastern philosophy reflected in many ancient Asian and African practices discovered within the Shaolin Temple's philosophy or ancient Timbuktu's Islamic schools of thought, schools based on this conceptual model are designed to advance human behavior, cultural practices, scholarly perspectives (Shujaa 1994). Intelligence is not simply measured from abstract results or assessment data points. Rather, education or the practice of becoming educated was nurtured and unraveled for some time prior to it manifesting. Indeed, people in these societies were not seen as intelligently wise or mature until they had experienced life reaching the age of forty (Shujaa 1994). In addition, children were seen as part of their experiences and could never become disconnected from them. So in a way, social-emotional and cultural learning made up a greater part of a person's cognitive ability rather than a separate part of their reality.

FHIA's classroom settings and environment are creatively designed, which seems to appeal to learners desires to want to learn. Anyone visiting the school lobby or auditorium can tell learning is taking place. The curriculum in Marcus's school remains rigorous and creatively constructed making students very proficient in the areas of reading, writing, and arithmetic.

Students learn Kiswahili, demonstrating fluency and literacy skills in the language. Many African scholars believe Kiswahili should become the national language for African Americans similar to Jews linguistically possessing Yiddish and Hebrew as their cultural tongue (Shujaa 1994).

Assessments and benchmarks are advanced from students' current grade, meaning if they are in the second grade they learn third- and fourth-grade subject areas, which radically progresses and advances their academic skill development. However, an area of concern with this type of instruction surfaces, addressing diverse learner needs (Gardner 2009). Nevertheless, great success stories continue at FHIA as students continue to graduate, travel the world, read critical literacy, expand their historic memory, display their computation and mathematical development skills, and enact astounding maturity behavior for their age.

In years past I have visited several public schools in the Roseland community whereupon the behavior of students and faculty were abrasive, to say the least. From cursing in the hallways, interacting with badgering security personal, and disengaging behaviors normalized within these school environments, I have witnessed far too many parents and students dismiss the value of acquiring an education.

Without question, this is not the case at FHIA. Students are immersed into the environment and totally focused toward success. Marcus's teachers command respect, which helps students embrace FHIA's mission and African-centered core values. If I had young kids living near this school community, I would make every effort to have my children attend FHIA so they could achieve a high-quality cultural education. I'm not the only one who believes this point, because FHIA continues to expand and grow, beating the odds of what success versus failure appears living in a hub city. Besides creating more schools similar to Marcus's vision, Chicago public schools continue to develop charter and contract schools in these areas that seek to replace public schools. Despite their intentions to develop successful educational models, they continue to struggle with connecting and teaching this population. To counter this, more freedom schools are necessary versus the district attempts to create philanthropic educational institutions.

The Village

Parents continue to seek resources and sophisticated schools to address the academic needs of their children. Besides placing their children into schools that appear as "cultural ghost towns," they continue to push back and fight for better school choices. This is none more evident than in the way "The Village" got its start almost ten years ago. Two families, led by Anita Hutchinson and Nakisha Hobbs, took the initiative to pull their children out of public schools to home school them.

Home schooling is another form of enacting a freedom-school concept where parents teach their children at home rather than having them attend a public institution. In this capacity, parents create a well-designed schedule, one that rivals modern-day schooling schedules, to teach their children. Quite often, a home-schooling parent has to place his or her career on hold to develop the time to educate the children. These parents attend workshops and conferences and purchase instructional resources and tools (Grant and Ray 2009). They radically relearn various subject areas to teach their children. In addition, they develop a sophisticated nutritious dietary plan distinctly different and far healthier than traditional schools (Grant and Ray 2009).

Hutchinson and Hobbs's home-school efforts became such a success they eventually welcomed and invited other parents on this journey to participate in a home-school network. Parents apart of the homeschool network were ethically and professionally diverse, allowing their network to reach a variety of parents located in various parts of the city. Several parents held professions as financial advisors, college professors, or grant writers, which made it all the more possible for the school to fundraise, obtain grants, and develop a viable donors' contact list. As a result, their home-school network grew into something fantastic, causing them to require more space. Eventually, they found that space in the south loop of Chicago inside an apartment complex known as River City.

At one point in time, the south loop existed as a hub city prior to the city's redevelopment initiatives. Fanciful apartment buildings along with a matrix of well-established businesses soon grappled this city's terrain making the south loop become a quaint, bourgeoisie geographic space. The school location for Hutchinson and Hobbs was perfect as parents living in the south loop struggled to find nearby primary schools that met their family's educational needs. It should be stated that African American and Latino parents are not the only families or groups of people struggling to find quality schooling for their children.

In a way, it is kind of ironic that whites find themselves torn by the district's creation of select enrollment or magnet schools, as they were once referred, because these schools were entirely developed to provide middle-income white families with viable educational options to remain in the city; otherwise, white families would uproot themselves to flee to neighboring suburbs (Lipman 2011).

Not only does the space capacity in select schools eventually run out, but these schools are exceptionally difficult and very competitive to get into. Students require a ninetieth percentile score on each of the core areas of the standardized achievement test to receive entry (Wetli and Riley 2014). Some select schools now require a ninety-ninth percentile score in the areas of reading and math to qualify for entry. Students must have all As, with few exceptions, before even applying. Many scholars believe this has created a three-tier educational system, with schools at the top acquiring all of the resources since they list the "premier" students in their enrollment records, and second- and third-tier institutions receive moderate to few reserves (Lipman 2011; Watkins 2011; Ravitch 2014).

Next to analyzing a country's gross domestic product index (GDP), Chicago public schools residing within a third tier or poor periphery zone similarly receive minimum investments besides receipt of a charter or contract school (Ravitch 2014). Many white parents find themselves forced to leave the city when their children cannot attend a high-quality charter or public school such as a Walt Disney, Walter Payton, Gwendolyn Brooks College Prep, or Northside College Prep, to name a few.

Schools designed in this fashion serve as nothing but miniature oligarchs dwelling across the city flushing working and middle-income hard working children to either attend a charter or contract school, run from the city, or deal with an underfunded, resource deprived traditional arrangements. Hutchinson, Hobbs, and other families saw the same thing, which resulted in them creating their own school to provide a safe harbor and protector to other families famished from corporate and elitist school ventures.

Village Learning Academy's "real genius" lies in its ability to have a diverse parent and student body. Not only do African American parents attend this free space zone, but also white, Asian, Jewish, and Latino families have formed a unique collective bond to educate their children here. Together they have created a fabulous school that allows parents to become "real" stakeholders and direct investors with their children's education and have a say about what students need to learn. At the Village one can see parents volunteering to teach classes, fundraise, and recruit students to this school community. In addition to volunteering at the school, parents plan and schedule international tours and trips for students and teachers. The parents' expertise, education, and involvement have truly helped to expand the school's existence. Although fundraising efforts remain critical to help the school's future, donors make up an intricate part of the school success because they deal with the business side of education allowing parents to primarily concentrate energy toward their children's learning. As a result, Village Leadership Academy showcases some of the best elementary scores on standardized tests and highest enrollment into Chicago's "elite" high schools and the nation's top colleges (Chicago Great Schools 2015).

Children, similar to those attending Marcus's school, are taught to think outside the box and not rely on rote-learning methods. The academic spaces are composed of rich literature, well-equipped computers, and other resources to nurture students' growth and development. Class sizes are small permitting teachers to work one on one with students, which strengthen learners' ability to master subject information. Instruction also possesses no boundaries as students learn advanced subjects within their grade levels. There is a guest speaker series that invites local politicians to visit classrooms to discuss topics that vary from community challenges to pivotal global affairs.

Since the school bases itself on the idea that their students are the next global leaders, they are taught how to community-organize and present proposals to develop grassroots campaigns. More importantly, students are immersed into a critical pedagogy that empowers their responsiveness and insightfulness to come up with solutions as counters to social maladies. Not surprising students and parents digest the school's norms and core values, which make them especially relish the atmosphere of learning and education. It is no wonder The Village ranks as a premier freedom school in this study and a noted model of what education, school choice, and community schooling should look like in the future.

Where Do We Go from Here?

The real challenge for parents, educators, and students is finding suitable domains where they can enjoy an academic space without the intrusion of political and private forces. There existed a time where schools were autonomous, secure, and a long-term career option for many idealistic professionals entering the field. This is not the case any longer. Many teachers, if they survive six years in the current climate, are viewed as survivors versus stakeholders. Teacher workloads or instructional responsibilities continue to increase as their pay remains stagnant, which exhausts an educator's hope to remain in the profession. Besides becoming a veteran to a school where former or graduating students can visit their alma mater to see their "old" favorite teachers, they journey from school to school every two to three years seeking an educational home (Ravitch 2010).

Although starting a school is an arduous task, to escape these "oppressive arenas" and once again cherish public or community schools educators, parents, and community leaders need to develop their own schools. Some would suggest this is far too radical an idea, but several Chicago schools exist, most notably independent frameworks, that developed new learning paradigms to combat this matter (e.g., Betty Shabazz Elementary, Dusable Leadership Academy (DSL), Barbara Sizemore, and Johnnie Coleman Academy).

However, these schools found it difficult to financially manage their institutions, especially paying their teachers a fair and equitable salary with health benefits, which led them to eventually turning their schools into charter or public structures to hire more skilled and experienced professionals. Without having a strong and consistent donor network, similar to colleges with strong alumni, these schools are forced to seek alternative funding mechanisms to support their existence.

Some private, political, and public forces argue schools' autonomy and unions invariably caused their input because so many public schools failed the tax paying public. Since the publication of *Nation at Risk* in 1983, schools have been under a microscope determining their level of effectiveness (Ravitch 2014). A school success now rests with its ability to perform sufficiently on the infamous standardized test, which measures an educator's effectiveness to apply and teach a "packaged curriculum" to students. This not only allowed the politics of corporate zeal to takeover schools, but also diminished educators' influence over their profession. No other occupation exists where employees specialized and trained to manage their industry become overtaken or controlled by an outside entity. Physicians, lawyers, trade professionals, firefighters, police, and other labor specialists monitor and establish the norms and policies of their profession. Many colleges or university systems empower professors to establish policy, curriculum, evaluation protocols, and assessment measures, and administration operates itself along the lines of supporting these educators' plans. The emergence of freedom schools, an old-school way of pushing back against private-public and elite schooling practices, is an effective way to transform the lives of educators, parents, and students.

How should teachers, parents, and students go about this task of transforming schools to their benefit? First, parents and educators should unionize a partnership to develop an educational plan for the children within these communities. Recently displaced and retired educators living in neighborhoods serve as a valuable assets and desire alternative instructional environments, regardless of the initial pay, where they can return back to the field they love. A special energy and vibrancy will soon surface causing people to seek their counsel, tutorial advice, and instructional spaces for their children to attend.

Similar to Marcus Kline's Freedom Academy, he sought community support and educator advice prior to establishing his institution. A viable educational plan and curriculum emerged that reflected what the community desired and intended for their children to learn rather than him imposing his educational vision onto the community. Also, a well-noted community tutorial agency originated in Chicago similarly along these lines, called Gregg Tutorial, located in the Hyde Park community. Started by several retired educators who were former home-school practitioners, they created space inside one of their residences to provide a home-school network to parents and neighborhood students with academic supports and advantages, transitioning into traditional school environments. Gregg Tutorial continues to achieve great use of community resources and participation to supply a clientele eager to learn and focused to achieve. Their results are telling and one of the best-kept secrets in education as they continue to transition exceptional students through Chicago's elite charter and public schools. Again, this mission began by educators and home-school specialists undertaking the task of developing transformative spaces for students of color to achieve in education.

Goal number two: The community, along with former educators, needs to acquire formerly closed school spaces, abandoned homes and buildings, or businesses, similar to the way private developers and investors locate ideal geographic areas or sites, and consolidate their money to purchase such properties. This will engineer new grounds to develop sites tailored away from the corporate model, turning schools over to the community. After all, schools belong to the taxpaying public and not private investors. Why should the public continue to pay for schools they really have no say in what goes on? In fact, Chicago public schools are most recently auctioning off or selling empty school buildings to businesses or organizations seeking property. Here again goes an excellent chance for the community to come together to form partnerships with educators frustrated by the "system" and on the verge of another labor strike to create independent schools. Community committees and consultative groups need to emerge from the educational "darkness" hovering over public schools and formulate strategies to develop building proposals to submit to the Chicago Public Schools (CPS) district to acquire these empty school buildings that taxpayers still have to pay for.

A recent investigative study suggests closed schools cost millions of dollars of upkeep and extended service because of several factors including

- depilated school buildings that require maintenance and structural support so they do not completely fall apart from water leakages, plumbing issues, electrical damages, or other hidden property damages that erode a building structure;
- sophisticated monitoring and policing of the buildings that remain to protect the properties from "stripping" by scavengers in need of materials, piping, or electrical parts; thus, the schools are guarded by high tech alarms and sophisticated gate systems that must be kept up and garner a huge bill to prevent break ins;
- heating costs that remain high, especially with Chicago's winters, making it necessary to heat these building so that frozen piping and water issues will not occur; and
- high appraisal and renovation costs accrued prior to selling the locations to public or private entities (Smyser and Roger 2014).

Also, some educators, parents, and students became so disgusted by the closing of their schools they intentionally damaged the buildings tearing electrical wire out of the ceiling while also destroying cafeteria spaces and bathroom utilities (Smyser and Roger, 2014). All of this costs major money for CPS to complete prior to marketing and selling their vacant institutions to the public or another owner. So in a way, it was easier for CPS to do what R&B legend Johnnie Taylor suggests it's cheaper to keep her.

This idea or concept is nothing new as Booker T. Washington upon leaving Hampton University with the support of Samuel Armstrong set out to discover a location to develop a freedom school to educate his fellow brothers and sisters that had just escaped slavery vestiges. Washington forward himself on a journey through parts of the south, especially Alabama, to find a geographic space to manage a freedom school. Eventually he found an empty former plantation with a modest building seemingly worthy enough to run a schoolhouse. Together with a few hands, skilled laborers, and nearby residents, he cleared the land, cutting down weeds, plowing the field, fixing up the structure, and making it ready for future students at minimum cost. If Washington could achieve these types of results in the late-1870s, why can't people of color do the same thing today? There are many unemployed and retired people living in communities ready and willing to contribute to their children's future. They are just as tired and fed up by the system as the adults working in the schools. They just need a push or planned attack, similar to Washington's idea of schooling, to support such an initiative. Instead of educators trying to find another school to survive in, they need to organize themselves away from the union and create partnerships with community residents.

When organized teachers seek to develop collaborations with local businesses, community activists, and parents, they are empowering their future as educators and role models to neighborhoods to take a stance on the important issues afflicting them. They further empower communities and neighborhoods exploited far too long while pushing back against the corporate educational matrix. After teachers leave work, they should meet twice a week at local community houses or centers and come up with a plan on how they will meet with community activists, clergy, and parents to identify potential properties to purchase to develop a school.

Like Hutchinson and Hobbs did, organized teachers and parents should make use of the community resources and expertise that compose these areas. Not only could this plan employee people from the community to cook the food, provide security, a custodial staff, maintenance workers, and paraprofessional teacher supports, but also refresh financial capital of people living in these areas. Many of these same folk often seek work in CPS's corrupt contract-riddled environment, where monies and job bids go to connected folk. CPS remains entrenched in financial crisis after crisis and fiscal scandal after scandal simply because it mismanages and misappropriates its funding. New charters schools are being built with new staff despite the district always crying broke. As a recent study reveals, a lot of school contracts, investments, and vending licensure continue to go to friends of the administration rather than the responsible people living in the school communities who can do the work at efficient costs (Catalyst Chicago 2014). In other words, it is more affordable to hire people in the community who are unemployed skilled laborers rather than constantly paying the same folk who cost the district an arm and a leg. After all, who receives the paper contract to supply the school? Which company or agency gets the bid to supply the food or janitorial services? How about the distribution of technical equipment, such as fax machines, Xerox machines, or computers? It usually is not people from the community but the same companies and private investors receiving the contract. Minority bids and contract acquisition remain at an all-time low despite the mayor's promise to turn the tide and diversify who gets what jobs. In reality, a new school should mean job opportunities for a community; however, it doesn't, and people that usually work in the school live outside the neighborhood and are in no way, shape, or form connected to the people they educate.

Educators establishing collaborative meetings and sessions with parents and students from the community would mean they

- develop a curriculum that the community needs;
- supply a community labor pool to fix up, secure, and maintenance the school; and
- create business and donor partnerships that will fundraise and support the new school initiatives.

Many communities are in need of having a curriculum that teaches their children how to become entrepreneurs, business investors, trade smiths, and truck drivers along with studying the arts and becoming athletes. The community needs to say what they expect their children to learn, so they should have a say about what goes on in the classroom. In this fashion educators become re-empowered to deliver knowledge to parents and children. Educators from here can construct environments that become teacher-parent-community driven institutions. Teachers can receive public tax dollars to manage their own schools, departing away from the eminent domain clause monopolized by CPS, to forward their tax dollars into a community school they control rather than leaving it up to the hands of zealots that have ruined education.

When schools first arose in this country, they surfaced as community frameworks where people could teach their children the ABCs of education: reading, mathematics, and writing. Of course, society has become more sophisticated and technologically driven over the years, but people should not run away from idea of what schools were originally intended to do. Schools exist to serve communities and the greater society with knowledgeable people who can add a little more to the next generation. The best examples of effective schooling are found in areas or pockets of the country where schools are connected to the community core beliefs and values. Typically, educators exist as a fabric of these school communities because their children attend or attended these schools, live near the school, know the parents, and have an investment as taxpaying citizens.

Examples of this are found in Dupage County, Chicago's northwest suburb, in communities of Naperville, Wheaton, Glenbard, and Lisle. A charter or contract school does not exist in these environments, and people from here refuse their services, arguing or contending such schools take tax dollars away from public students. Clearly, they want a say about how their tax dollars are being spent to fund their schools.

Chicago and many other major cities surpassed this idea long ago and remain bent on making schools more about private development rather than community-based houses. Private investors are exploiting the struggles to educate African American and Latino children by establishing schools that do not reflect their community or educational desires. The emergence of freedom schools will create radical new approaches to counter the current private wave out to exploit and destroy public schools, their communities, and educators who teach black and brown children.

Away from Home

Today, I remain an educator teaching special needs learners while serving as an assistant professor at a state university. Years have flashed by remembering what personal transformations and transitions I have went through to make it to this point. Thus far, I have enjoyed six years teaching diverse learners helping them to improve upon their reading, writing, and math skills along with strengthening their academic plans and organizational development. Such work brings with it great satisfaction as you watch students graduate to take on life's next journey. I have also watched a number of colleagues disappear from the profession, either leaving it altogether or finding another school to take on a different set of challenges or achieve a better working climate. My greatest joy comes from teaching at the collegiate level where I work as a professor in the college of education, providing students with strategies and techniques to advance their knowledge in their chosen profession. I not only inform them as to what to watch out for but also what to avoid and how to address their dilemmas entering the field. I have worked with several student teachers and educators in the classroom aiding and assisting their efforts to buttress their careers and specialization. I especially love to share my research, literacy resources, and methodology to enhance their inquiry and discovery investigations to find materials and lessons to better engage students.

Yet with almost twenty years in the field, I find myself perplexed from the struggles most educators find themselves encountering: How do I remain strong to survive the present course of where public education is headed? Boy, do I miss working in schools that once belonged to the community.

Turnover is so great at the current high school where I work that I will have had four principals headed into my seventh year with an average teacher attrition rate of two years. Sometimes I feel the only reason I remain a teacher in this system is to have connections to students, supply my family with additional financial support, and stay abreast of the current school issues prevalent in the field. That way I can assuredly communicate with my college students the inner workings of the profession while staying attuned to the realities happening in the classroom. I understand clearly how teachers are overworked and stressed by the amount of everyday responsibilities and workloads they must take on to function in the classroom.

As mentioned earlier, a lot of teachers are just surviving the challenges education has directed to them from budget cuts, excessive evaluation, over-testing, directives for robotic teaching methods, communication issues with administrators, overprotective and enabling parents, and students' social-emotional challenges occurring in the classroom. There is certainly a fear to being a classroom teacher these days, and the reward or pleasure of teaching has long gone away from the field.

Veteran teachers, like myself, are more expendable than ever before because of our credentials, years in the profession, and educational perspectives frighten those managing the system. What do I mean by this? Most educators, after ten years, have witnessed a lot in schools. They understand deeply how education works and know things constantly change for the "supposed better."

When I first started this profession, I remember one teacher informing me that education cycles every five years. Meaning the people outside education are always trying new things or methods to improve student and teacher performance. He or she indicated to me if I stuck around long enough, I would find the things these experts dismissed as outdated would return as a new concept or idea down the road. Boy, was this person right! Teachers who have been in the field for a length of time are not only experienced but also incredibly wise about how things "really work." Nothing, at this point, surprises them. That is why when the policyholders or administrators attempt to talk down to teachers as though they do not understand or know what is happening, it insults educators' intelligence. Teachers are some of the smartest and brightest people a person would want to run across and should receive respect and appreciation for having knowledge about their craft. But they are not, and that is why teachers are questioning the operation of things especially as it pertains to what should go on in a classroom. Besides working with this very smart and wise professional population, the managers and officials running schools continue to subordinate their intellectual capital developing procedures and instructional protocols that dismiss educators' professional expertise.

As mentioned before, I really believe the system cannot keep performing at the rate it is today and remain intact. A lot of researchers constantly discuss the issues or challenges with school inequity but never bring up the teacher inequities that exist throughout the nation (Kozol 2012). Here in Illinois, depending on the district, a teacher's salary is tied to property tax, which is totally unfair. Teachers, regardless of the school district, have to pass the same tests and classes to receive their credentials; however, if they work in a poor district they receive less money. It really should exist the other way around where people working in the most challenged districts earn more. Educators should receive the same money per state since public teaching is a government held post. The inequities found with salaries alone are driving people from the profession and having effective teachers avoid or leave poorer districts. As such, the teaching numbers continue to drop as the professional standards increase. A number of districts have a lot of empty teaching positions because they cannot find enough certified educators to fill this void.

The numbers have especially gone from bad to worse for African American males in the profession. There was a time African American males were seen as superintendents, principals, math instructors, history teachers, or counselors. However, if you find an African American male in today's classroom, a person is staring in the face of a dinosaur. As Kunjufa's (2002) research has always emphatically suggested black boys need black men as role models with which to identify. However, as Kunjufu's research points out, the men usually found in school environments are janitors, food service providers, or disciplinarians versus classroom teachers, administrators, or superintendents. So black men can cook, clean, and scare kids to act right or else, but they cannot educate and lead children. Every child, not just African American boys, need to know African American men are smart, brilliant, dedicated, and responsible for helping educate children. To not have students see this remains a bigger problem in today's schools. It also speaks to the lack of investment and dedication society continues to forward to African American males, their communities where they live, or the children they raise. Low teaching numbers, along with the plight of African American male teachers, have led a number of districts to recruit from various non-teaching professions and academic programs that grant temporary licensure.

Gary, Indiana, for example has most recently declared teachers do not require teaching classes if they pass the educational tests required to receive certification (McInerny 2014). What kind of madness is this that a teacher does not have to take any method or subject area courses, but all they have to do is pass a test and they become qualified to teach? This further demonstrates how desperate districts are becoming to hire teachers in the classroom because so many dedicated professionals are fleeing from schools.

Collegiate programs also have introduced stricter requirements to acquire a teacher certification, which adds more pressure to an existing field challenged to find quality and dedicated professionals. Most recently the federal government legislated edTPA for education college programs to apply to strengthen their monitoring of effective educational practices. edTPA uses multi-assessment and evaluative approaches of a student teacher's performance as they seek certification. One of the ways they do this is video recording an instructor's lesson as they seek certification. Prospective teachers are randomly recorded by a state agency to determine if they meet the licensure requirements. Depending on how effective or challenged the student teacher performs on that particular day, edTPA evaluates them despite whatever instructional outcomes are produced (Ravitch 2013).

Many districts and unions remain contentious about this form of evaluation because like most professionals, an unseasoned or novice instructor could just be having had a "bad day in the classroom." Student teaching is hard and varies from day to day, especially depending on the type of classroom a novice instructor inherits. Simply put, student teachers require a lot of consistent support and assistance throughout their journey. It is a little harsh leaving a person's certification up to one classroom experience or instructional interaction. Yet to receive current teacher accreditation, under the present scrutinizing forces controlling education, from their perspective this is a practical solution to weave out incoming poorly prepared instructors. Imagine if every intern professional received one official, unbeknownst recording to qualify entry into their field. Would people say this is fair-minded professional practice? Besides new police officers being videotaped when encountering minorities, a necessary clause for years of illegal practices, I am not certain most people would view this as an acceptable practice. But I'm not sure about a whole lot of things these days in education.

The fact remains people studying to become teachers are finding it ever the more difficult to receive credentials to enter the field. As a result, a lot of college programs are struggling to keep their doors open to attract people into this profession (Ravitch 2013). Whatever is driving people away from education these days must be addressed, or this nation will have a serious teacher shortage on their hands. Poor pay, steeper credential requirements, stricter classroom standards, and harsher professional evaluative measures must be corrected if we are ever going to improve education.

How Long Will I Remain?

A question constantly scurries through my mind: How much longer can I remain in this field? Most certainly, I see myself teaching college classes as an older gentleman writing articles and publishing a few more books dealing with cultural studies or best practices, yet I become depressed when thinking about my tenure as a public school teacher working with youth. Burnout is becoming clearer for me these days, and it has nothing to do with the students I teach. Rather, the nature of bureaucratic policies, poor administrative practices, teacher attrition, over-testing, helicopter parenting, and constant scrutiny make it harder to stay in this profession. Believe me when I say this: money is not the major factor of why I and other educators love to teach. Although money serves as a great influencer and extrinsic reward, most teachers enter the profession because they truly believe they can make a difference in the lives of others. Teachers are some of the best people a person can want to know because we love interacting with and helping people. We enjoy working with students, parents, and communities. I know I'm not speaking alone when discussing this matter.

Most recently I had the privilege of sitting down with a retired principal and school leader of more than forty years along with three recently retired teachers to discuss this very same subject. All of them stated that I needed to hold on as best as I could, and when possible flee public education.

As one educator mentioned, "The public schools really do not respect or want blacks around anymore in education. They feel strongly white teachers are the better-qualified candidates to educate Black children." All of the research says the contrary speaking to how diversity and teacher role-modeling for children remains critical for all age groups (Kunjufu 2002; Shujaa 1994; Kozol 2012).

So the notion that these educators strongly feel public education has kicked Black educators to the side is disturbing. However, similar to what has already been mentioned, I feel the same way. Many of the schools struggle to relate to teachers period, white or black. Yet as history has proven time and time again, African Americans along with other minorities usually are the last ones to receive any fair treatment or practices when it comes to their issues. My race has had to fight for everything, and it seems to never stop.

The retried principal further mentioned that the practices and current trends in education do not come from educators, but from people outside the field making it harder to service students. Who is better to know what the profession requires other than the people working in it everyday? Parents and teachers should exist on one accord to work together to streamline the necessities and best practices of education. Again, this text strongly advocates for community schooling versus private-pubic school entities managing education. Since their involvement in education, turnover, burnout, and lower salaries within the profession continue to increase causing less people to want to become teachers.

When I first started education, it was a delight and idealistic dream to make a difference in the lives of young people and the communities where they lived. Although many educators continue to impact students and help inspire them to achieve, far too many teachers are not appreciated for the work they perform. Maybe a national strike will get people and this country to understand educators' value and strength in this economy. Also, it might change the way schools are managed, returning the power of teaching back into the hands of the parents and educators.

The quest for change is necessary if we are to ever improve the way schooling practices are developed and managed in this country. When people can see the greater good and value educators truly make on the lives of others, teaching will once again become enjoyable for countless educators and me.

BIBLIOGRAPHY

2Pac. *Makaveli: The Don Killuminati*. Koch/Death Row, 1996.

Ali, S. and M. Ryan. "Merging and Creating Culturally Relevant Pedagogy in Public Education," *Journal of Research Initiatives*, 1 no. 1 (2013), 40–6.

Alexander, M. *The New Jim Crow*. The New Press, NY, 2010.

Anderson, J. *The Education of Blacks in the South, 1860-1930*, 1st ed. North Carolina: University of North Carolina Press, 1988.

Asane, MK *It's Bigger Than Hip Hop: The Rise of the Post-Hip Hop Generation*. New York: St. Martin's Griffin, 2009.

Bell, C. C., and EJ Jenkins. "Traumatic Stress and Children," *Journal of Health Care for the Poor and Underserved*, 2, (1991) 175–88.

Bennett, L. *Before the Mayflower*, 6th revised ed. New York: Penguin Press, 1993.

Bloom, J. and WE Martin. *Black against Empire*. Berkeley, CA: University of California Press, 2013.

Bowles, S. and H. Gintis. *Schooling in Capitalist America: Educational Reform and the Contradictions of Economic Life*, 2nd ed. Chicago: Haymarket Press, 2011, 21.

British Literature. Excerpt from *Beowulf* translated by Burton Raffel. Viking Penguin, 1963, 2008.

Buckingham, D. *Youth, Identity, and Digital Media*. Cambridge, MA: The MIT Press, 2007.

Cannon, R. Parents Sue to Halt Chicago School Closings Alleging Discrimination. In These Times: With Liberty and Justice For All, retrieved on July 25, 2013, from http://inthesetimes.com/working/entry/15349/parents_sue_cps_over_alleged_discrimination.

Carp, S. Minimal Cost Savings for Closing Schools: Analysis. Catalyst Chicago: Independent Reporting on Urban Schools, retrieved on October 31, 2012, from http://catalyst-chicago.org/2012/10/minimal-cost-savings-closing-schools-analysis/.

Carroll, R. *Uncle Tom or New Negro? African Americans Reflect on Booker T. Washington and up from Slavery 100 Years Later.* New York: Broadway Books, 2006.

Carruthers, J. *Intellectual Warfare.* Chicago: Third World Press, 1999.

Catalyst Chicago. Staff. Budget Cuts, Teachers of Color, No Bank Claim. In Catalyst Chicago: Independent Reporting on Urban Schools, retrieved on July 16, 2015, from http://catalyst-chicago.org/2015/07/take-5-budget-cuts-teachers-of-color-no-bank-claim/.

Catalyst Chicago. Staff. Black Chicago By the Numbers. In Catalyst Chicago: Independent Reporting on Urban Schools, retrieved on November, 20, 2014, from http://catalyst-Chicago.org/2014/11/black-chicago-numbers/.

Catalyst Chicago. Staff. Uno Charter in Question? In Catalyst Chicago: Independent Reporting on Urban Schools, retrieved on September 2014 from http://catalyst-chicago.org/2014/09/take-5-karen-lewis-questions-uno-and-irs-kennedy-king-honor/.

Center for Public Education (n.d.). How many students with disabilities are in our schools? Retrieved from: www.data-first.org/data/how-many-students-with-disabilities-are-in-our-schools/.

Clay, A. *The Hip Hop Generation Fights Back: Youth, Activism, and Post-Civil Rights Politics.* New York: New York University Press, 2012.

Chicago Great Schools. Great Schools City Rating. Retrieved June 16, 2014. from http://www.greatschools.org/illinois/chicago/.

Chicago Public Schools. School Data Report. Retrieved on February 6, 2015 from http://www.cps.edu/schooldata.

Cohen, R. How Philadelphia Charter Operator Can Spend Tens of Thousands of Public Dollars to Fight a Union. In The American Prospect, retrieved on June, 4, 2015, from http://prospect.org/article/uphill-battle-unionizing-philly-charter-school.

Cooley-Strickland, M., Quille, T. J., Griffin, et al. "Community Violence and Youth: Affect, Behavior, Substance Use, and Academics," *Clinical Child Family Psychological Review*, 12, no. 2 (2009), 127–56.

Crawford, B. *Writin' Dirty: An Anthology*. New York: Byron Crawford, 2014.

Cronon, ED and Franklin, JH. *Black Moses: The Story of Marcus Garvey and the Universal Negro Improvement Association*. Wisconsin: University of Wisconsin Press, 1960.

Crouch, JL, RF Hanson, BE Saunders, et al. "Income, Race/Ethnicity, and Exposure to Violence in Youth: Results from the National Survey of Adolescents," *Journal of Community Psychology*, 28 (2000), 625–41.

Delpit, L. *Other People's children: Cultural Conflict in the Classroom*, 2nd ed. New York: The New Press, 2006.

Denzin, NK and YS Lincoln, eds. *Handbook of Qualitative Research*. Thousand Oaks, CA: Sage, 2011.

Denzin, NK, YS Lincoln, and L Tuhiwai Smith, eds. *Handbook of Critical and Indigenous Methodologies*. Thousand Oaks, CA: Sage, 2008.

Dewey, J. "Individuality and Experience." In *The Later Works of John Dewey, 1925–1953, Vol. 2, 1925–7:Essays*. Carbondale: Southern Illinois University Press, [1925-1927] 1984.

Delpit, L. *Multiplication Is for White People: Raising Expectations for Other People's Children*. New York: The New Press, 2013.

Dimitriadis, G. *Performing Identity/Performing Culture: Hip Hop as Text, Pedagogy, and Lived Practice*, 2nd ed. New York: Peter Lang, 2009.

Dimitriadis, G. *Friendship, Cliques, and Gangs: Young Black Men Coming of Age in Urban America*. New York: Teacher College Press, 2003.

Douglas, E. and R. Crowson. *Shaping Education Policy: Power and Process*. New York: Rutledge, 2011.

Douglass, F. *Narrative of Frederick Douglass*. New York: Dover Publication, 1995.

Du Bois, WEB. *Souls of Black folks*, 3rd ed. New York: Dover, 1994.

Dufour, R. and R. Eaker. *Professional Learning Communities at Work: Best Practices for Enhancing Student Achievement*, 1st ed. New York: Solution Tree, 1988.

Emdin, C. *Urban Science Education for the Hip Hop Generation*. Rotterdam, The Netherlands: Sense, 2010.

Evanzz, K. *The Messenger: The Rise and Fall of Elijah Muhammad*. New York: Vintage, 2011.

Fernandes, S. *Close to the Edge: In Search of the Global Hip Hop Generation*. New York: Verso, 2011.

Foucult, M. *The Foucult Reader*. New York: Vintage Press, 1984.

Forman, M. *That's the Joint!: The Hip Hop Studies*. New York: Routledge, 2011.

Freire, P. *Pedagogy of the Oppressed*, 30th anniversary ed. New York: Continuum, 2000.

Gardner, H. *Five Minds for the Future*. Boston: Harvard Business Review Press, 2009.

Gebert, A. and M. Joffee. *Value Creation as the Aim of Education*. New York: Rowman and Littlefield, 2007.

Garvey, A. *The Philosophy and Opinions of Marcus Garvey: Africa for the Africans*, 2nd ed. New York: Routledge, 2013.

Grant, KB and JA Ray. *Home School and Community Collaboration: Culturally Responsive Family Involvement*. New York: Sage, 2009.

Tsunesaburo Makiguchi andAndrew Gebert (2013). New York:Routledge.

Gillborn, D. and G. Ladson-Billings. *Critical Race Theory*. New York: Routledge, 2009.

Giroux, H. *On Critical Pedagogy*. New York: Continuum, 2011.

Goldstein, D. (January, 13, 2009). Charter Schools and Segregation. In the education policy and analysis archives from http://epaa.asu.edu/ojs/article/viewFile/779/878analysis archives Volume 19, Number 1.

Greendfield, E. and J. Pickney. Mary McLeod Bethune (1994). New York: Harper Collins, retrieved from http://prospect.org/article/charter-schools-and-segregation.

Gwynne, SC. *Empire of the Summer Moon: Quanah Parker and the Rise and Fall of the Comanches, The Most Powerful Indian Tribe in American History*. New York: Scriber, 2011.

Hernstein, R. and C. Murray. *The Bell Curve*. New York: First Press Book, 1994.

Hill, ML. *Beats, Rhymes, and Classroom Life: Hip Hop Pedagogy and the Politics of Identity.* New York: Teacher College Press, 2009.

Hill, ML and E. Petchauer. *Schooling Hip Hop: Expanding Hip Hop Based. Education across the Curriculum.* New York: Teacher College Press, 2014.

Hinduja, S. and JW Patchin. "Bullying, Cyberbullying, and Suicide," *Archives of Suicide Research,* 14 (2010) 206–12.

Hing, J. Activist Say No to Another School Desert' in Chicago. Color Lines News for Action. Retrieved on Dec, 4, 2013, from http://www.colorlines.com/articles/activists-say-no-another-school-desert-chicago.

Horne, J. *Breach of Faith: Hurricane Katrina and the Near Death of a Great American City.* New York: Random House, 2006.

Ignatiev, N. *How the Irish became White* (1st edition). New York: Routledge, 2008.

Jackson, P. Educate or die. *Black Star Publication,* IV, 1-4, 2010.

Janesick, V. *"Stretching" Exercises for Qualitative Researchers.* New York: Sage, 2010.

Johnstone, A. and E. Terzakis. "Pedagogy and Revolution: Reading Freire in Context" in Jeff Bale and Sarah Knopp, eds. *Education and Capitalism: Struggles for Learning and Liberation.* Chicago: Haymarket Press, 2012, 187–210.

Karp, S. CPS Declines to Release Data on Select Enrollment, Sets Aside More Seats for Minority Students. In Catalyst Chicago: Independent Reporting on Urban School, retrieved on March 2010 from http://catalyst-chicago.org/2010/03/cps-declines-release-data-selective-enrollment-sets-aside-more-seats-minority/.

Kitwana, B. *The Hip Hop Generation.* New York: Basic Civitas, 2002.

Kozol, J. *Savage Inequalities: Children in American Schools.* New York: Broadway Books, 2012.

Kozol, J. *The Shame of a Nation: The Restoration of Apartheid Schooling in America.* New York: Broadway, 2006.

Kunjufa, J. *Conspiracy to Destroy Black Boys: Volume II.* Chicago: Black Printing Press, 1987.

_____. *Black Students. Middle-Class Teachers.* Chicago: African American Images, 2002.

Ladson-Billings, G. *The Dreamkeepers: Successful Teachers of African American Children.* San Francisco: Jossey-Bass, 1994.

_____. *Beyond the Big House: African American Educators on Teacher Education.* New York: Teacher College Press, 2005.

Larson. E. *The Devil in the White City: A Saga of Magic and Murder at the Fair That Changed America.* New York: Vintage, 2004.

Latif, N and S. Latif. *Slavery: The African American Psychic Trauma.* Chicago: Latif Communications Group Inc, 1994.

Lee, C. *Culture, Literacy, and Learning: Taking Bloom in the Midst of the Whirlwind.* New York: Teachers College Press, 2007.

Lil Wayne. "God Bless America." *I am not a Human Being II.* DLX. EX. Cash Money, 2013.

Lipman, P. *The New Political Economy of Urban Education: Neo Liberalism, Race, and the Right to the City (Critical Social Thought).* New York: Routledge, 2011.

_____. *Race, Class, and Power in School Restructuring.* Albany: State University of New York Press, 1998.

Lubiano, W. *The House That Race Built: Original Essays by Toni Morrison, Angela Y. Davis, Cornel West, and Others on Black Americans and Politics in America Today.* New York: Vintage, 1998.

Lupe Fiasco. *Real (Food & Liquor),* recorded by Atlantic, 2006.

National Basketball Association. (n.d.). George Gervin Biography. Retrieved June 2012 from http://www.nba.com/history/players/gervin_bio.html.

Nas. "Black President." New York: Columbia Records, Def Jam Recording, 2008.

Marble, M. Malcolm X: A Life of Reinvention. New York: Penguin Books, 2011.

McAdam, D. Freedom Summer. UK: Oxford University Press, 1990.

McInerney, C. Controversial Teacher Licensure Requirements Will Move Forward. In State Impact: Education From the Capital to the Classroom. Retrieved on September 3, 2014, from http://indianapublicmedia.org/stateimpact/2014/09/03/controversial-teacher-licensure language-move/.

McInerney, L. What the Difference between Charter Schools and Free Schools? In *The Guardian,* retrieved on July 15, 2013, from http://www.theguardian.com/education/2013/jul/15/ us-charter-school-answerable-community.

Morrell, E. and J. Duncan-Andrade. "Toward a Critical Classroom Discourse: Promoting Academic Literacy through Engaging Hip Hop Culture with Urban Youth," *English Journal*, 91 no. 6 (2002), 88–94.

Ogbu, J. *Black American Students in an Affluent Suburb: A Study of Academic Disengagement (Socio-Cultural, Political, and Historical Studies in Education)*. New York: Routledge, 2003.

_____. "Understanding Cultural Diversity and Learning," *Educational Researcher*, 21 no. 8 (1992), 5–14.

_____. *Minority Education and Caste: The American System in Cross Cultural Perspective*. New York: Academic Press, 1978.

Omi, M. and H. Winat. *Racial Formation in the Unites States from the 1960s to the 1990s*, 2nd ed. New York: Routledge, 1994.

Parker, K. "Instructions for the Hip Hop Scholar." In K. Parker's *Instructions for the Hip Hop Scholar*. New York: Brooklyn Press, 2013, 1–30.

Perry, T. and L. Delpit, L. *The Real Ebonics Debate: Power, Language, and the Education of African-American Children*. Boston: Beacon, 1998.

Perry, T., C. Steele, and A. Hilliard III. *Young, Gifted, and Black*. Boston: Beacon, 2003.

Postman, N. *Amusing Ourselves to Death: Public Discourse in the Age of Business*. New York: Penguin Books, 2005.

Public Enemy. *He Got Game*. New York: Island Records, Def Jam Recordings, 1998.

Ravitch, D. *Reign of Error: the Hoax of the Privatization Movement and the Danger to America's Public Schools*. New York: Vintage, 2014.

Ravitch, D. Blog. What Is edTPA and Why Do Critics Dislike It? Retrieved on June 3, 2013, from http://dianeravitch.net/2013/06/03/ what-is-edtpa-and-why-do-critics-dislike-it/.

_____. *The Death and Life of the Great American School System: How Testing and Choice are Undermining Education*. Philadelphia: Basic Books, 2010.

Rihanna. "Pour It Up." *Unapologetic*. New York: Island Records, Def Jam Recordings, November 19, 2012.

Rideout, VJ, UG Foehr, and DF Roberts. *Generation M2: Media in the Lives of 8-to-18-Year Olds.* Menlo Park, CA: Kaiser Family Foundation, 2010.

Rosa, M. and DC Orey, "Culturally Relevant Pedagogy: An Enthnomathematical Approach," *Horizontes,* 28, no. 1, 19–31, 2011.

Rose, T. *Black Noise: Rap Music and Black Culture in Contemporary America.* Middletown, CT: Wesleyan University Press, 2013.

Sandlin, JA, BD Schultz, and J. Burdick, eds. *Handbook of Public Pedagogy.* New York: Routledge, 2010.

Sergiovanni, T. *Moral Leadership: Getting to the Heart of School Improvement,* 1st ed. New York: Jossey Bass, 1996.

Shakespeare, W. *The Tragedy of Romeo and Juliet (Illustrated).* e-Book, Amazon Digital, 2014.

Shor. I. *Empowering Education: Critical Teaching for Social Change.* Chicago: University of Chicago Press, 1992.

Shujaa. M. *Too Much Schooling, Too Little Education: A Paradox of Black Life in White Societies.* New Jersey: African World Press, 1994.

_____. *Beyond Desegregation: The Politics of Quality in African American Schooling.* Thousand Oaks, CA: Corwin Press, 1996.

Shurgin, G. and KC O'Keeffe. "Clinical Report on the Impact of Social Media on Children and Adolescents," *Pediatrics,* 127 (2011) 800–4.

Smith, E., P. Jackson, B. Kitwana, and A. Pollard III. *The Hip Hop Church: Connecting with the Movement Shaping Our Culture.* Downers Grove, IL: InterVarsity Press, 2013.

Smith, S. *There Is no Next: NBA Legends Speak on the legacy of Michael Jordan.* Chicago: Division Publishing, 2014.

Smyser, K. and Rogers, P. Shuttered Schools Still Cost Millions, Are Targets For Vandalism: Acting President Of The Chicago Teacher Union Says CPS Officials Aren't Using "Real Math" When Talking About Cost Savings. In NBC Chicago Investigates Retrieved December 2, 2014, from http://www.nbcchicago.com/investigations/chicago-shuttered-schools-284361541.html.

Stovall, D. "We Can Relate: Hip Hop Culture, Critical Pedagogy, and the Secondary Classroom," *Urban Education*, 41 no. 6 (2006), 585–602.

Strauss, V. Chicago Charters Do No Better Than Traditional Public Schools, New Study Finds. In *Washington Post*, retrieved April 7, 2014, from http://www.washingtonpost.com/blogs/answer-sheet/wp/2014/04/07/chicago-charters-do-no-better-than-traditional-public-schools-new-study-finds/.

_____. What's Wrong with DC's Facilities/Charter Study? In *Washington Post*, retrieved February 2012 from http://www.washingtonpost.com/blogs/answer-sheet/post/whats-wrong-with-dcs-facilitiescharter-study/2012/02/12/gIQAdcnkTR_blog.html.

Stult, D. and S. Thomas. Teacher Turnover in Charter Schools. In National Center on School Choice (n.d.) Teacher Turnover in Charter and Traditional Public Schools. Retrieved from http://www.vanderbilt.edu/schoolchoice/blog/?p=155.

Sullivan, A. M. Pursuit of goals in partnerships: Empowerment in practice. Paper presented at the Australian Association for Research in Education International Education Research Conference, Brisbane, Qld. Retrieved from http://www.aare.edu.au/02pap/sul02098.htm, 2009.

Swerdlow, S. *How Segregated Is Chicago, and Does it Matter? Chicago Sun Times*, retrieved May 27, 2014, from http://chicago.suntimes.com/politics/7/71/165325/how-segregated-is-chicago-and-does-it-matter.

Tyler, RW. "Specific Approaches to Curriculum Development." In J. Schaffarzick, and D. Hampson *Strategies for Curriculum Development*. Berkeley CA: McCutchan, 1975, 256.

Tupac Shakur: *In Order to Choose Your Path*. Research and Develop (blog), accessed August 15, 2013. blog.researchdevelop.org/post/58374429412/tupac-shakur-in-order-to-choose-your-path.

Watkins, W. *The Assault on Public Education: Confronting the Politics of Corporate School Reform*. New York: Teacher College Press, 2011.

Watkins, W. *The White Architects of Black Education: Ideology and Power in America, 1865–1954*. New York: Teacher College Press, 2001.

Wetli, P. and Riley, C. Getting Into City's Elite Middle School Programs Tougher Than Ever. In Pilsen, Little Village News. Retrieved April 8, 2014, from http://www.dnainfo.com/chicago/20140408/near-west-side/lane-tech-whitney-young-early-entry-programs-more-competitive-than-ever.

Wiltz, T. Black Unemployment Challenges States. In the Pew Charitable Trusts Retrieved June 9, 2015, from http://www.pewtrusts.org/en/research-and-analysis/blogs/stateline/2015/6/09/qa-black-unemployment-challenges-states.

Wong, HK. *The First Days of School: How to Be an Effective Teacher*, 4th ed. New York: Harry K. Wong Publications, 2009.

Zirin, D. *Game Over: How Politics Has Turned the Sports World upside Down*. New York: The New Press, 2013.

Printed in the United States
By Bookmasters